Dolls

CHARLES SCRIBNER'S SONS · NEW YORK

1 3 5 7 9 11 13 15 17 19 I/C 20 18 16 14 12 10 8 6 4 2

Printed in Great Britain

Library of Congress Catalog Card Number 78-21747

ISBN 0-684-16124-9

Introduction

Making dolls is an enchanting craft that can be quite simply childs-play – providing hours of enjoyment at very little cost and with very little equipment.

Dolls provides clear instructions and diagrams which will enable you to make every imaginable kind of doll – from rag to costume, from miniature to life-size, and from those requiring little more than patience (such as the pipecleaner dolls) to those that take a little more skill (such as the Russian canvaswork dolls).

There are also ideas and instructions for making different types of doll's houses – from cloth, polystyrene, or wood – and for making matchbox furniture to fit inside.

Yet dolls are not only for children, and in *Dolls* you will also find the type of doll you need to set the theme for a collection – perhaps from those in historical dress, inspired by painted portraits.

Contents

Simple
stitch dolls

Rag doll

Soft cloth dolls made of cast-off clothes and odds and ends from the sewing basket are a part of childhood's fondest memories. Easy and inexpensive to make, mothers through the centuries and all over the world have lovingly stitched these simple playthings for their children.

Doll's body
Pattern pieces overleaf.
The finished doll is 60cm (24in) high.

Making the doll's body
Enlarge pattern pieces from graph on page 8. A seam allowance of 1cm (⅜in) is included on the pattern where necessary. In calico [cotton material] cut one head front, two head backs, two body sections, and cut two legs and two arms on the fold. Cut all pieces on the straight of grain. Mark point and top of dart with single tailor's tacks.

Cut four shoe uppers [tops] in black felt, two soles and two eye centres in brown felt, two eye whites in white and a mouth in pink. With right sides facing, tack and stitch head back sections from A to B. Trim seam, clip curve and press open. With right sides facing, tack and stitch the dart in head front. Press dart to one side. Tack and stitch head front to head back, with right sides together and matching darts to centre back seam, easing where necessary. Trim seam and turn head through to right side. Fill firmly and oversew [overcast] raw neck edges together.

To make hair, loop wool backwards and forwards across head, back stitching to head along line of dart and down centre back seam. Start stitching on face 2.5cm (1in) below seam line (fig.1) and continue to 4cm (1½in) above neck edge at back. At the back of the head pull strands evenly across head and back stitch to side seam at each side, beginning 2.5cm (1in) above neck edge and finishing 4cm (1½in) from centre line of back stitch (fig.2).

Tie hair and trim ends.

With right sides facing, tack and stitch one arm on the stitching

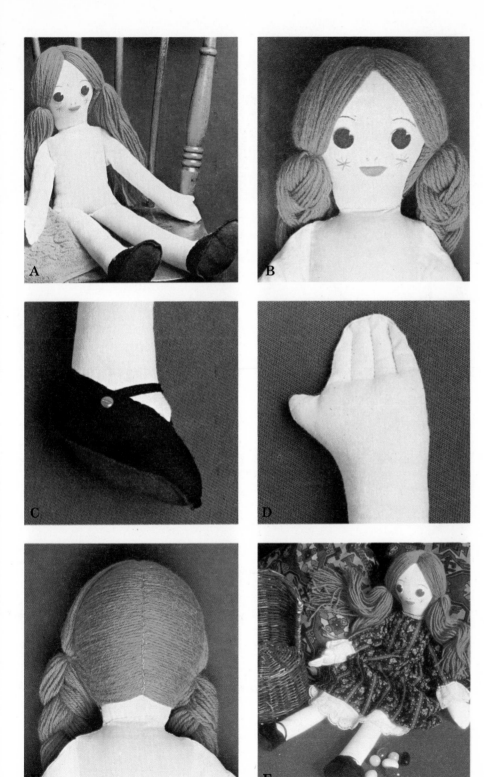

A. Finished doll, undressed.
B. Doll's face (hair can be plaited [braided] if preferred).
C. Shoe with strap.
D. Lines for fingers machine stitched.
E. Hair back stitched to centre back seam.
F. The clothed doll.

7

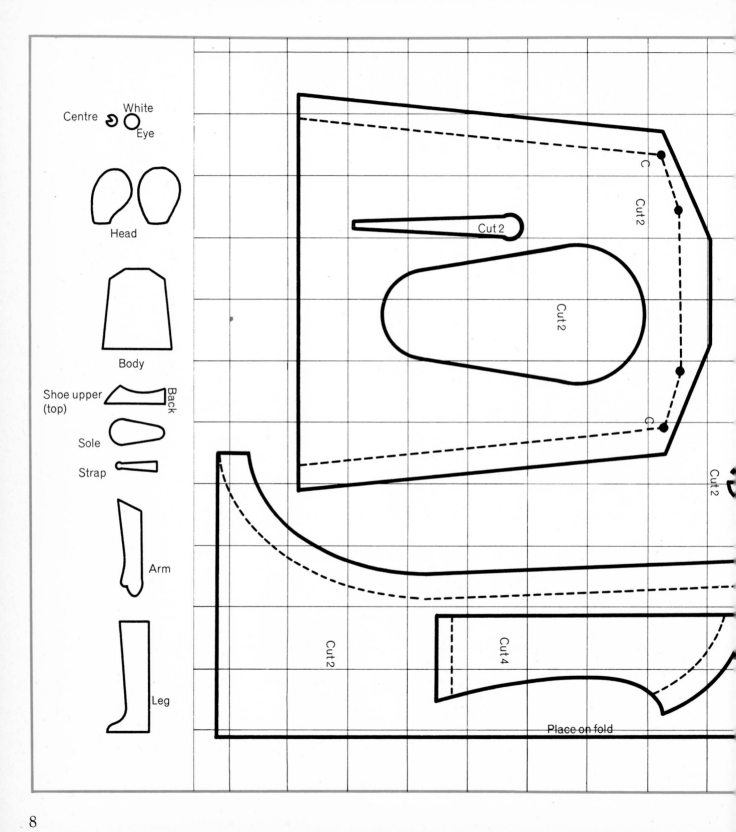

Centre   White   Eye

Head

Body

Shoe upper (top)   Back

Sole

Strap

Arm

Leg

Cut 2

Cut 2

Cut 2

Cut 2

Cut 2

Cut 4

Place on fold

C

C

Graph patterns
Each square = 2.5cm (1in) sq.

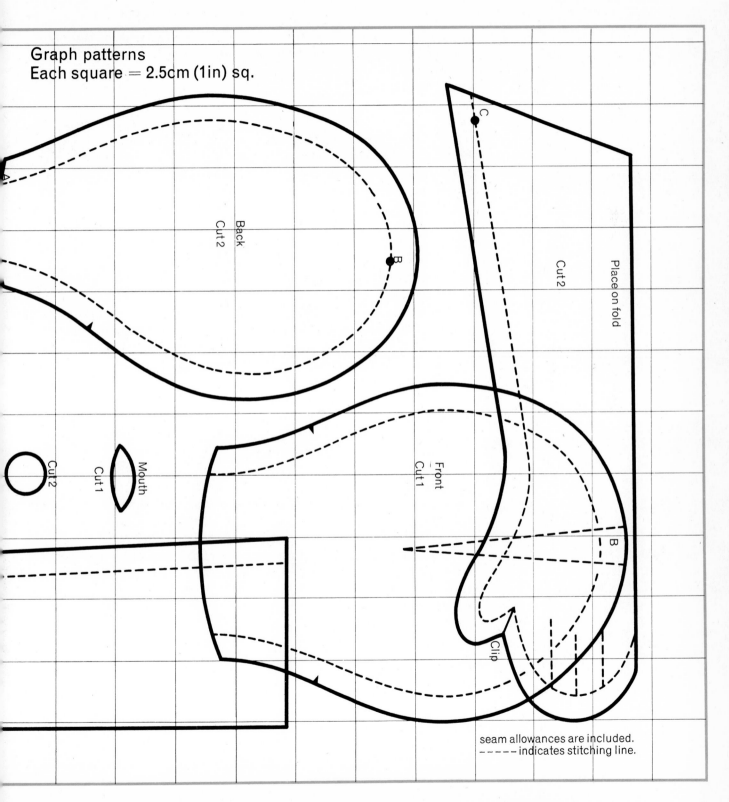

Back
Cut 2

B

A

C

Place on fold

Cut 2

Mouth
Cut 1

Cut 2

Front
Cut 1

B

Clip

seam allowances are included.
------ indicates stitching line.

line. Trim, clip into angle of thumb and turn through to right side. Lightly fill the hand and machine stitch lines for fingers. Fill arm firmly to within 2.5cm (1in) of the top. Machine stitch across the tops 1cm ($\frac{3}{8}$in) from the raw edge. Make up the other arm in the same way.

Place two body sections with right sides together and place one arm between them. Match raw edges and points C. Tack and stitch the side seam from C to bottom (fig.3). Repeat with the other arm.

Stitch shoulder seams. Turn through to right side.

Turn in raw neck edge on body and insert head about 1.3cm ($\frac{1}{2}$in) into opening, matching side seams on head to shoulder seams on body. Tack and then oversew [overcast] the body to the head (fig.4). Fill body firmly to within 4cm ($1\frac{1}{2}$in) of lower edge.

Turn in 1cm ($\frac{3}{8}$in) along the lower raw edge and tack temporarily to close.

With right sides together, stitch back seam of one pair of shoe uppers [tops] 6mm ($\frac{1}{4}$in) from the edge. Press seam open and trim. With right sides up, place top edge of upper [top] over bottom edge of one leg, overlapping by 1.3cm ($\frac{1}{2}$in). Tack and topstitch by hand or machine 3mm ($\frac{1}{8}$in) from edge of upper [top]. (You may have to stretch the felt slightly.)

With right sides together stitch leg and front seam of shoe as one. Trim seam, clip curve on leg and turn through to right side.

Back stitch sole to shoe upper [top] 3mm ($\frac{1}{8}$in) from the edge, leaving one side open to enable filling to be pushed into the leg from the foot as well as from the top of the leg.

Fill leg firmly to within 2.5cm (1in) of the top. Push filling down from the top with a knitting needle if necessary.

Back stitch sole opening and machine stitch across top of leg with seam at centre front, stitching 1cm ($\frac{3}{8}$in) from the raw edge.

Work two rows of machine stitching along the length of one shoe strap and oversew [overcast] to shoe. Stitch a button at outer end of strap.

Make up the other leg in the same way.

Remove tacking from lower edge of body.

Insert legs into body opening, so that raw edges are about 1.3cm ($\frac{1}{2}$in) inside the body.

Tack and back stitch across lower edge of body with two rows of stitching, one close to the edge and the other about 1.3cm ($\frac{1}{2}$in) up from the edge (fig.6).

Stitch centre of eye to white (fig.7).

Arrange eyes and mouth on face and sew in place. Embroider eye brows and nostrils and then 'stars' for cheeks.

1. Back stitching for hair starts 2.5cm (1in) below seam line.
2. Back stitching on side seam starts 2.5cm (1in) above neck edge.
3. Arm stitched inbetween two body pieces.
4. Body oversewn [overcast] firmly to head.
5. Shoe upper [top] stitched to leg 3mm ($\frac{1}{8}$in) from the edge.
6. Legs inserted into body and then stitched.
7. Assembling the eye.

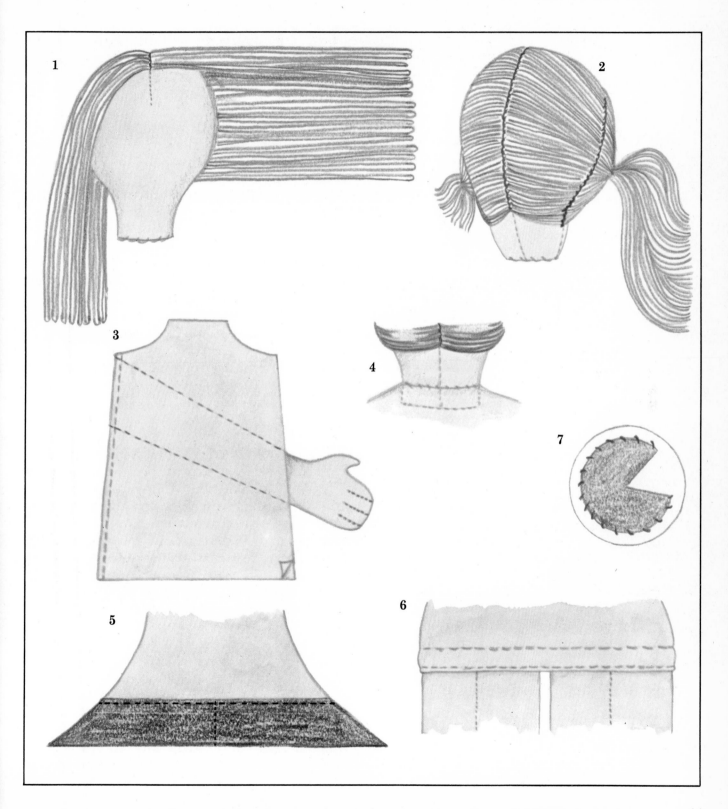

Rag doll wardrobe

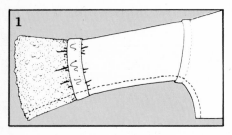

1. Lace, sleeve seam and bodice side seam stitched in one operation. Opposite: Washing day!

Here are trace patterns and the instructions for making a whole outfit – dress, petticoat and panties – for the rag doll.

Dress

Trace off the pattern for the bodice and sleeves.
From printed cotton cut a piece for the skirt 74cm × 27cm (29in × 10$\frac{1}{2}$in) then, cut out two sleeves, two bodice back pieces and then one bodice front on the fold.
With right sides facing, tack and stitch front and back bodice together at shoulders.
Run a gathering thread along the top of each sleeve 6mm ($\frac{1}{4}$in) from the raw edge. Pin sleeves to armholes of bodice, with right sides together and matching the shoulder seams to centre top of each sleeve. Pull up gathers to fit. Tack and stitch.
Turn 3mm ($\frac{1}{8}$in) and then 1.5cm ($\frac{5}{8}$in) on bottom of each sleeve to wrong side. Tack and stitch close to edge of first fold.
Cut two pieces of 5cm (2in) wide lace to fit the bottom edges of the sleeves and topstitch in place along the very edge of each sleeve.
Cut two pieces of elastic 11.5cm (4$\frac{1}{2}$in) long and thread through the casings you have just made and secure the ends.
With right sides together and matching at all points, tack and stitch raw edges of lace, sleeve seam and bodice side seam in one operation (fig.1). Trim seams to 6mm ($\frac{1}{4}$in) and neaten [finish] together. Repeat with the other side.
With right sides facing, stitch the two short edges of skirt piece together to within 10cm (4in) of one long edge (waist edge). Mark side and centre front of top of skirt with single tailor's tacks or pins. Run a gathering thread along top edge of skirt 1cm ($\frac{3}{8}$in) from the edge. Pin skirt to bodice, with right sides together, pulling up gathers to fit. Tack and stitch. Press seam up on to bodice. Turn 3mm ($\frac{1}{8}$in) and then 6mm ($\frac{1}{4}$in) on either side of back opening to the wrong side. Tack and stitch close to first fold.
Cut a 2.5cm (1in) wide bias strip in printed cotton to fit the neck, plus a little extra for seams. With right side of binding to wrong side of bodice, tack and stitch the strip to the neck edge. Trim

seam allowance to 6mm ($\frac{1}{4}$in).

Trim raw ends to 6mm ($\frac{1}{4}$in) and turn to wrong side of bias strip. Turn bias on to right side of bodice. Turn under 6mm ($\frac{1}{4}$in), tack and topstitch close to lower edge of bias. Slip stitch the ends. Slip stitch the 1cm ($\frac{3}{8}$in) lace around the neck on the stitching line, turning in and neatening [finishing] the ends.

Attach buttons to left side of bodice back and make buttonholes in the other side to correspond.

Alternatively, attach press studs [snap fasteners].

Turn 3mm ($\frac{1}{8}$in) and then 1.5cm ($\frac{5}{8}$in) to wrong side at lower edge of dress and slip stitch the hem.

Petticoat

Cut a strip of white lawn 74cm $\times$ 24cm (29in $\times$ 9$\frac{1}{2}$in).

Turn 1cm ($\frac{3}{8}$in) on one long edge to the right side and press (this is the bottom edge of the petticoat).

Cut a piece of broderie anglaise [eyelet] 74cm (29in); pin it to the right side of the bottom of the petticoat. The lower edge of the insertion should be just above the folded edge of petticoat.

Tack and stitch along both edges of the insertion, thus enclosing raw edge of petticoat.

With right sides together, tack and stitch seam and broderie anglaise [eyelet] in one operation. Neaten [finish] seams.

On the waist edge turn 3mm ($\frac{1}{8}$in) and then 1.3cm ($\frac{1}{2}$in) to the wrong side. Tack and stitch close to the first fold, leaving a 2.5cm (1in) opening for inserting elastic. Cut a piece of elastic to fit the doll's waist, thread it through the casing and oversew [overcast] the ends together securely. Slip stitch the opening.

Panties

Trace off the pattern for the panties and cut two pieces in lawn on the straight of grain.

Cut a piece of broderie anglaise [eyelet] to fit each leg edge, including seams (four pieces in all).

Turn 6mm ($\frac{1}{4}$in) on one leg edge to right side and press. Attach one of the pieces of broderie anglaise [eyelet] to cover the raw edge as for bottom of petticoat. Repeat with other three leg edges.

With right sides together, tack and stitch the side seams, stitching short ends of broderie anglaise [eyelet] in the same operation. Neaten [finish] seams.

With right sides together, tack and stitch the crotch seam and broderie anglaise [eyelet]. Trim seams to 6mm ($\frac{1}{4}$in) and finish. Make casing and insert elastic at top of panties as for petticoat. Turn finished panties through to right side.

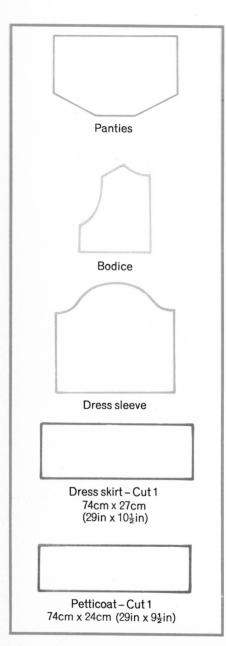

Panties

Bodice

Dress sleeve

Dress skirt – Cut 1
74cm x 27cm
(29in x 10$\frac{1}{2}$in)

Petticoat – Cut 1
74cm x 24cm (29in x 9$\frac{1}{2}$in)

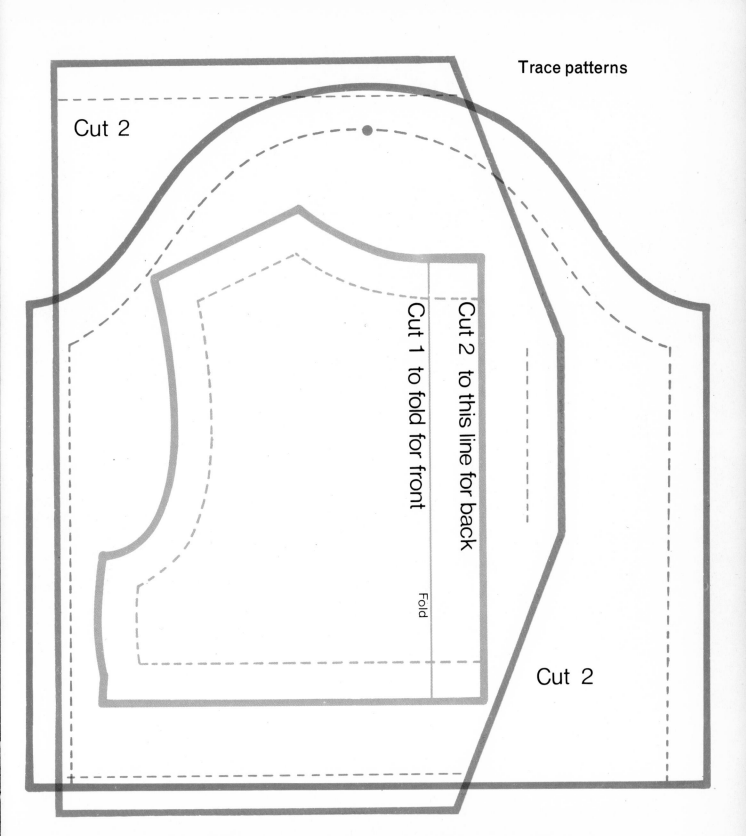

Trace patterns

Cut 2

Cut 1 to fold for front

Cut 2 to this line for back

Fold

Cut 2

15

Wool doll

Wool doll 35cm (14in)

You will need:
Two 50gm (2oz) balls double
knitting wool in a natural colour.
One ball mohair-type brown wool
for hair.
Child's hollow plastic playball
roughly 18cm (7in) circumference.
Scraps of red felt for mouth and
non-woven interfacing for eyes.
Brown and black felt-tip pens.
Fabric adhesive.
1.3cm (½in) wide ribbon 25.5cm
(10in) long to tie hair.

*Right: The finished doll. Some
patterns for dressing her can be
found on pages 127-135.*

Making the doll

Arms Cut two 25.5cm (10in) lengths of natural wool for binding [tying] the arms.

Make a skein 40.5cm (16in) long and 100 strands thick. Cut the skein at each end and bind [tie] it with one of the lengths of wool about 2.5cm (1in) from one end (fig.1).

Body and legs Cut five 25.5cm (10in) lengths of natural wool for binding [tying] the body and legs. Make a skein 102cm (40in) long and 150 strands thick, cut the skein at each end and bind [tie] it firmly in the middle (fig.3). Lay the arms across the middle of the skein, fold the skein over them and then bind [tie] it firmly just below the arms to hold them in place.

Bind the skein again about 5cm (2in) further down to make the waist. From this point, divide the skein in half and plait [braid] each half to make the legs. Bind [tie] each leg firmly from each end. Trim the ends of the arms and legs into a neat shape.

Head Cover the plastic ball with fabric glue leaving a small space at the top and bottom so you can hold it between your thumb and forefinger.

Wind the wool round and round the ball taking care that all the strands go in the same direction and cross each other at the top and bottom. When the ball is completely covered, darn in the loose end of the wool to neaten it. Leave the head to dry completely.

Thread the darning needle with wool and sew the head to the body.

Face From non-woven interfacing cut two eye shapes and using felt-tip pens colour them in carefully and leave to dry.

From red felt cut the mouth shape. Glue this and the eyes onto head.

Use felt-tip pens to make the eyebrows, two dots for the nose and eyelashes.

Hair Cut 80 35cm (14in) lengths of mohair-type wool for the main bulk of hair and 20 7.5cm (3in) lengths of the same wool for the fringe [bangs]. Stitch the fringe [bangs] first. Taking four strands at a time, fold in half and sew onto the fringe [bang] stitching line. For the rest of the hair, once again taking four strands at a time, stitch through the centre along the stitching line.

Sew the grouped strands closely together so that the head does not show through.

When all the hair has been sewn, tie into pony tails. The back strands will be much too long but this does not matter as the pony tails need to be trimmed evenly.

Finally tie the pony tails with ribbon.

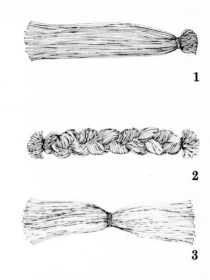

1

2

3

1. Cut the skein at each end and bind [tie] it firmly at one end.
2. Plait [braid] the skein and bind [tie] the remaining end.
3. The skein for the body and legs, bound [tied] firmly in the middle.

Life-size doll

Life-size doll

You will need:
90cm (35in) wide cream jersey:
age 8 years, 2.65m (2⅞yd): age 10
years, 2.75m (3yd).
90cm (35in) wide calico [cotton
material]: same lengths as for
jersey.
2½kg (5½lb) kapok.
Cardboard for soles of feet.
Embroidery thread, scraps of
fabric, felt tip pens or water
colours for features.
3 × 50gm (2oz) balls of wool for
hair.

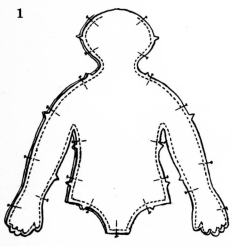

1

1. *An outline of the body,*
indicating where the pieces
should be pinned together.
Opposite: The finished life-size
doll holding a doll of her own.

Meet Maggie. Dress her up! Maggie's a life-sized playmate for an eight to ten year old because she can share in their wardrobe as well as in their games. Maggie's face can be painted or embroidered with a variety of features and her hair can be plaited [braided], tied up with ribbons or left loose.

Making the pattern

The pattern and instructions given here are for the equivalent measurements of an 8 or 10 year old. (See measurement chart with graph pattern.) Each size is indicated on the graph pattern by a cutting line of a different colour. Draw up the pattern to scale from the graph pattern given. One square represents 2.5cm (1in) square. There are no seam allowances included on the pattern. When cutting out add 1.3cm (½in) to all seam edges. Be sure to follow pattern layout and grain lines.

To make the doll

Before assembling the doll, tack the jersey pieces to the calico [cotton material] and treat as one fabric. Also, it is simpler to work the features on the face before making up [finishing].

Body

With right sides together and matching notches, pin the body pieces together, leaving 15cm (6in) free at the top of the head (fig.1). Stitch around the edge. Trim the seam and clip the curved edges.
Turn the body to the right side and press the stitched edges.
Stuff the body, arms and head, making sure that the measurements follow those on the chart. Sew up the opening securely.
Top stitch underarm to shoulder as indicated on the pattern. Top stitch the hand to the circles as on the pattern to form the finger shaping (fig.2).

Legs

With the right sides together and matching notches, pin the inside

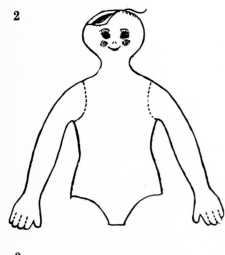

2

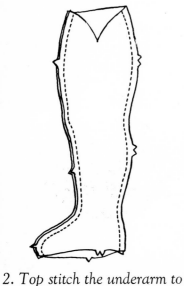

3

2. Top stitch the underarm to the shoulder.
3. Pin the inside leg to the outside leg. Stitch the seams and press open.

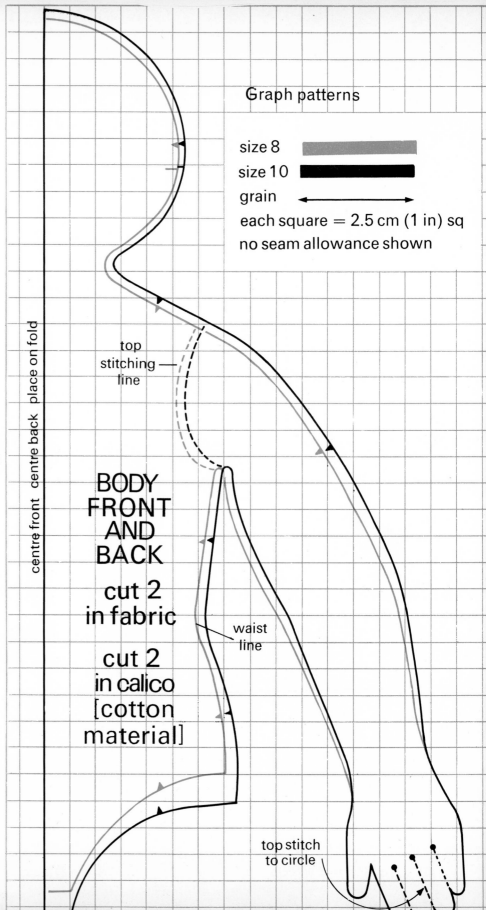

Graph patterns

size 8 ▬▬▬
size 10 ▬▬▬
grain ◄─────►
each square = 2.5 cm (1 in) sq
no seam allowance shown

centre front   centre back   place on fold

top stitching line

BODY
FRONT
AND
BACK

cut 2
in fabric

cut 2
in calico
[cotton
material]

waist line

top stitch to circle

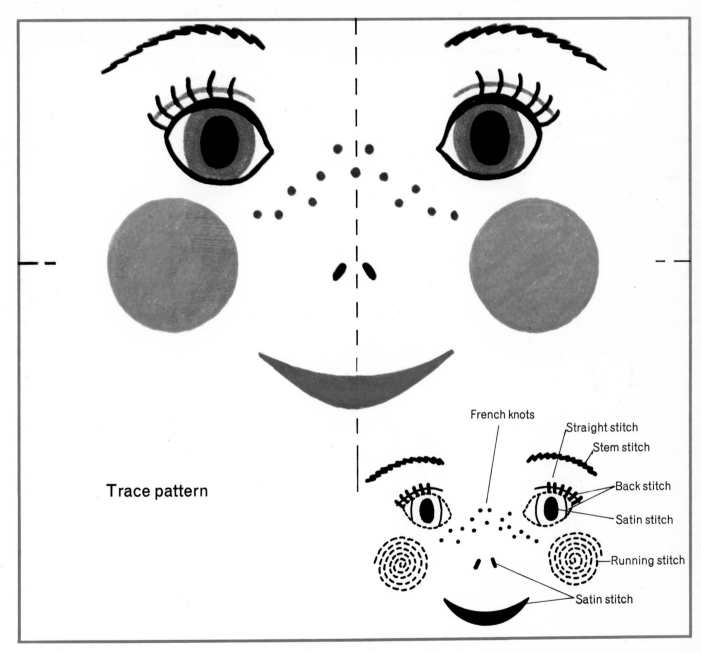

Trace pattern

French knots

Straight stitch

Stem stitch

Back stitch

Satin stitch

Running stitch

Satin stitch

the embroidery illustration, or they can be cut from felt or fabric and appliqued onto the face. It is simpler to do this before making up [finishing] the doll.

The features can also be traced or drawn lightly onto the face and filled in with coloured felt tip pens. Water colours may be used for a soft colour effect, but are more difficult to work with as they tend to run on the jersey.

Above: Some ideas for embroidering the face.

Japanese dolls

Opposite: The finished dolls in traditional dress. Precise instructions are given for matching every detail.

Use up off-cuts of exotic fabrics, rich braid trims, beads and sequins to create these dolls. fashioned on Japanese costumes. The mother wears a kimono held in place by a wide stiff sash, and the silver beads in her hair represent rice flowers. The son has an embroidered felt jacket, and both wear flat summer sandals.

To make the mother doll

Enlarge the pattern for the body to the correct size and cut out two body pieces in calico [cotton material]. Run a gathering thread along the top edge of the head. Allowing a 6mm (¼in) seam allowance all round, sew the two pieces together leaving a gap across the top of the head. Clip the curves and turn inside out. Stuff the body with kapok through the opening, tucking the raw edges inside before drawing the gathering threads tight and fasten off.

Using the trace pattern for the face, embroider the features with satin stitch and back stitch. Use a single strand of black, white, red, brown and mauve stranded cotton. Sew a line of running stitches to indicate the chin. Fasten off the stitches at the top of the head near the gathering line.

For the hair cut 25.5cm (10in) lengths of wool, fold them in half, and sew the folded ends to the head around the face and across the back of the neck. Separate the strands of wool and draw them all to the top of the head away from the face. Fold back, tuck the raw ends under and stitch the folded wool to the top of the hair (fig.1). Using the trace pattern, cut out two socks in white felt, two soles in blue felt, and two sandal straps in blue felt. Also cut out two soles in cardboard. Wrap one sock round each leg and sew, joining the front seams down the leg and foot. Stuff the socks with kapok. With a piece of cardboard inside each foot, sew the felt soles to the socks. Fold the straps in half and sew the folded end to each centre sole front. Sew the single ends one to each side of the soles so they curve over the doll's foot.

Enlarge the pattern for the petticoat to the correct size and cut out two pieces in printed cotton. With the right sides together, sew the

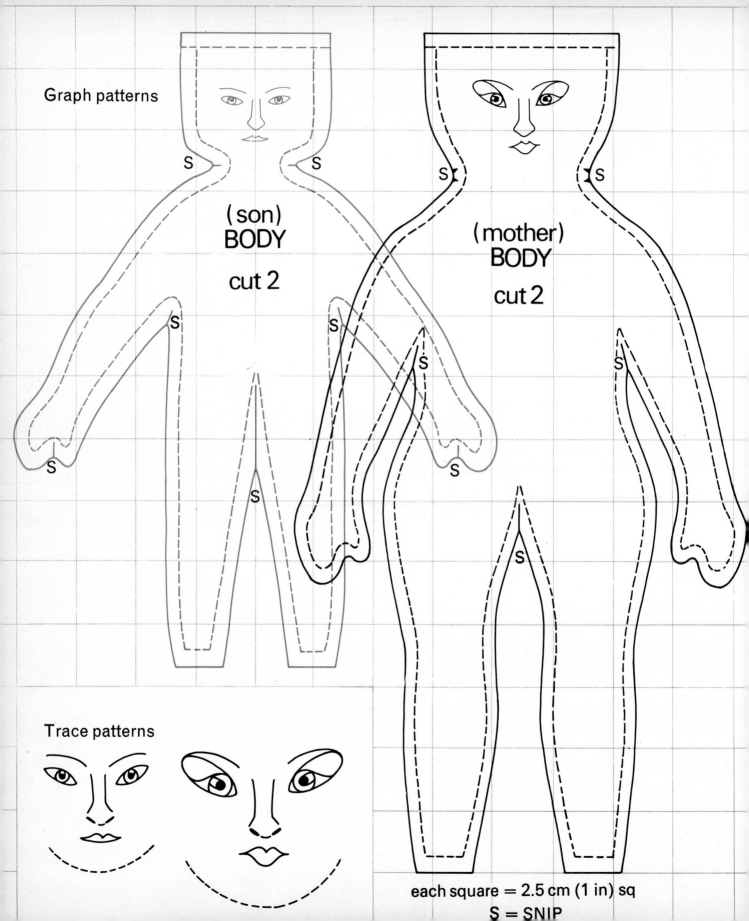

Graph patterns

(son)
BODY

cut 2

(mother)
BODY

cut 2

Trace patterns

each square = 2.5 cm (1 in) sq
S = SNIP

side seams. Make a 6mm (¼in) hem around the armhole opening and along the bottom edge of the petticoat. Join one shoulder seam. Cut a strip for the neckband in printed cotton measuring 12cm × 2.5cm (4¾in × 1in). Sew to the right side of the neck, fold over and hem on the wrong side. Turn the petticoat to the right side and press. Fit on the doll and oversew [overcast] the remaining shoulder with tiny stitches. Alternatively, this shoulder can be fastened with press studs [snap fasteners] to make the garment removable.

Draw the kimono pattern pieces to the correct size. Cut out pattern pieces in pink silk, positioning on folds as indicated.

Cut a strip in black silk measuring 19.3cm × 2.5cm (7½in × 1in) for the neckband. Sew a 6mm (¼in) seam down the centre back of the kimono to the bottom edge. Also, sew two 6mm (¼in) side seams, one from each armhole to the bottom edge. Sew 6mm (¼in) hems on the wrong side around each armhole edge, and join the shoulder seams with the right sides together. Make a 1.3cm (½in) hem along the kimono neck and down each side of the front. Match the centre of the neckband with the centre back of the kimono, with the right sides together. Make sure the edge of the neckband and edge of the kimono are level. Sew the neckband to the kimono, leaving 6mm (¼in) unsewn at each end of the band. Fold the material over to the wrong side of the kimono neck and hem. Tuck in the raw edges at the end of the band and oversew [overcast]. Sew a 6mm (¼in) hem round the bottom of the kimono.

Make a 6mm (¼in) hem along the two opposite sides of each sleeve piece. Fold each sleeve in half with the right sides together, and sew 6mm (¼in) seam along the short edge. Turn each sleeve to the right side and oversew [overcast] along the bottom end, to within 2cm (¾in) of the fold, to allow room for the hand to pass through. Match the sleeve fold with the shoulder seam and join the sleeves to the kimono, oversewing [overcasting] on the wrong side, for 2.5cm (1in) either side of the shoulder seam. Leave the remainder of the sleeve under the arm unattached. Sew the 6mm (¼in) wide braid round the bottom of the kimono, about 1.3cm (½in) above the bottom edge.

Follow the trace pattern to embroider the motifs with sequins on the front of the kimono, using chain stitch and satin stitch on the lower one. Press the finished garment and fit on the doll.

To make the sash cut a strip of printed cotton measuring 6.5cm × 19.3cm (2½in × 7½in). With the right sides together, fold in half lengthways and sew a 6mm (¼in) seam. Turn to the right side and press with the seam running along the centre inside of the band. Tuck in the raw edges at each end and oversew [overcast],

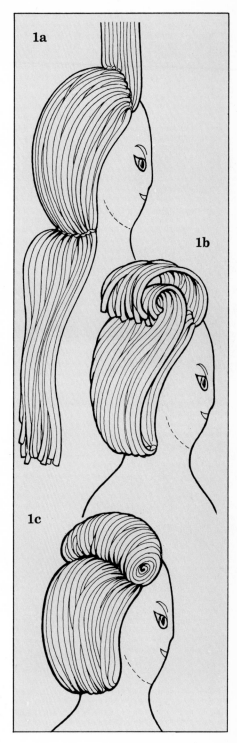

1a, b, c. How to style the hair.

27

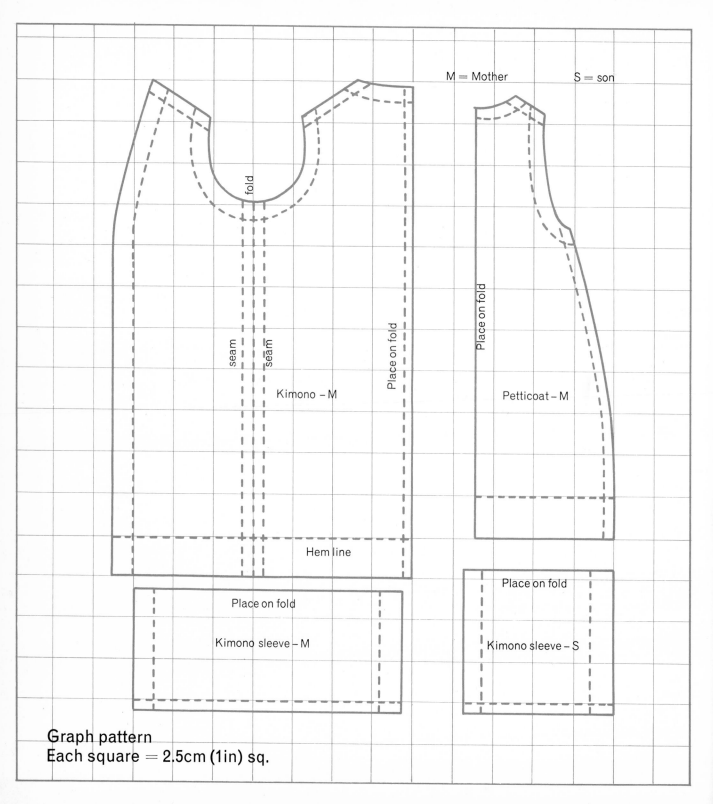

M = Mother   S = son

fold

seam   seam

Kimono – M

Place on fold

Petticoat – M

Place on fold

Hem line

Place on fold

Kimono sleeve – M

Place on fold

Kimono sleeve – S

Graph pattern
Each square = 2.5cm (1in) sq.

Trace patterns

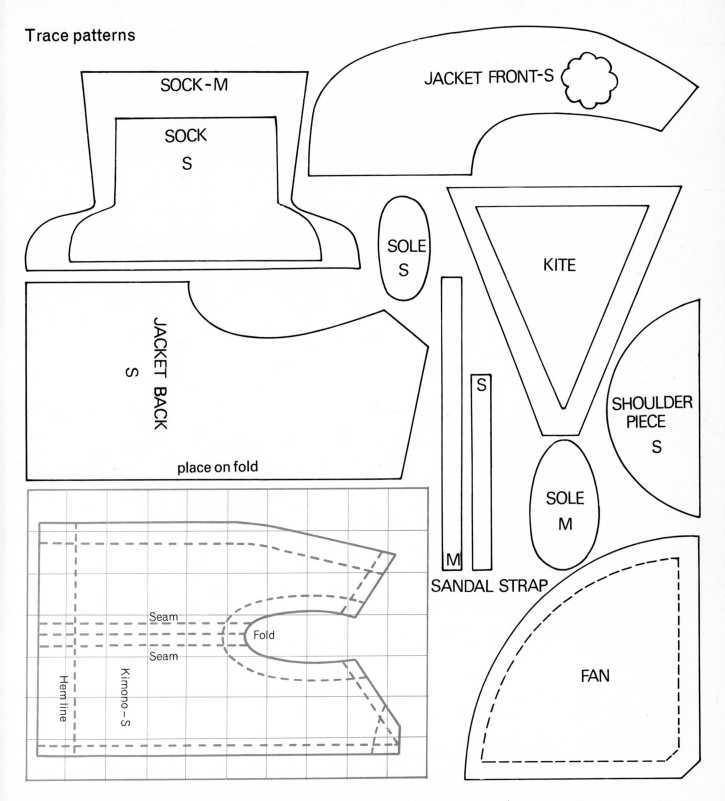

SOCK - M

SOCK
S

JACKET FRONT - S

JACKET BACK
S

place on fold

SOLE
S

KITE

SHOULDER
PIECE
S

SOLE
M

S

M

SANDAL STRAP

Seam

Fold

Seam

Hem line

Kimono - S

FAN

joining the two ends at the same time. Cut a 19.3cm (7½in) length of the 2cm (¾in) wide braid, place in the middle of the sash and oversew [overcast] with tiny stitches along both edges. Cut another strip of printed cotton measuring 28cm × 6.5cm (11in × 2½in) and make a band in the same way as the first. Wind the second band round your fingers twice, making sure the seam is on the outside.

This should leave a piece hanging unfolded, and the folded piece should measure 4.5cm (1¾in). Place in the centre back of the sash over the join, and stitch in the middle to hold in place.

Once this piece is secure, fold the remaining length in the opposite direction, wrapping twice round the folded piece and the sash together. Stitch down on the inside of the sash (fig.2).

Slide the sash over the doll's legs and position around the doll's middle with the bow at the back.

Using the trace pattern, cut out two pieces of printed cotton for the fan. With wrong sides facing, oversew [overcast] all three

2a, b. How to fold the sash.
3. Decoration for the front of the kimonos.
4. Chain stitch.
5. Satin stitch.

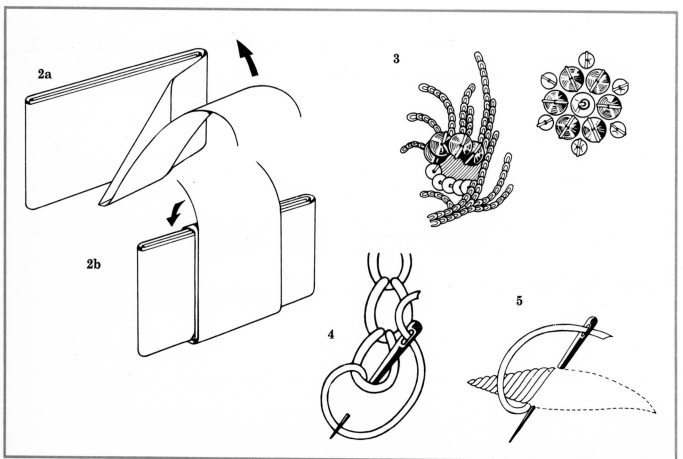

edges with tiny stitches. Decorate the rounded edge with sequins. Attach the fan firmly to the back of the doll's hand, with the sequins facing forward.

Make the rice flowers by cutting out two circles measuring 2.5cm (1in) diameter in pink silk. Using one circle, gather the round edge together and sew to the top right side of the hair, keeping the gathers underneath. String up three lengths of silver beads to measure 2.5cm (1in) each and sew to the middle of the silk, making sure the stitches go through to the hair. This also flattens the round of silk and the gathers should be well hidden. Repeat for the left side of the hair.

To make the son doll

Draw up the son's body pattern to the correct size and follow the instructions given for the mother's body.

Embroider the features in the same way as those on the mother doll, using the trace pattern for the son's face.

To make the hair cut 15cm (6in) lengths of wool and fold them in half. Sew the folded ends to the centre of the crown. Trim the wool all round the face and across the back of the neck. Using tiny stitches, catch the ends about 6mm ($\frac{1}{4}$in) from the hairline. Make the feet as for mother doll, using the trace pattern for the son's feet.

Draw the son's kimono pattern to the correct size, and cut out in printed cotton. Also cut a strip of pink silk for the neckband measuring 15.6cm × 2.5cm ($6\frac{1}{4}$in × 1in). Follow the instructions given for the mother's kimono. Press and fit on the doll. For the sash cut a strip of printed cotton measuring 48 cm × 3.2cm (19in × $1\frac{1}{4}$in). Fold lengthways with the right side out.

Turn the edges inwards and oversew [overcast] the whole length of the sash, including the ends, with tiny stitches. Press and fit round the doll's waist, tying in a bow at the back.

Cut out the son's jacket in blue felt. Join both shoulder seams and sew the shoulder pieces round the top half of each armhole. Sew the side seams from below the armhole to the bottom edge of the jacket. Decorate the edge of each shoulder piece with silver beads. Stitch the motifs in the same way as those on the mother's kimono. Using the outer kite pattern, cut out one piece in black silk and one piece in blue felt. Cut out the inner piece of the kite pattern in cardboard. With the cardboard between the blue felt and the black felt, oversew [overcast] the edges of all three together, tucking in the raw edges on the black silk. Decorate the silk with sequins. For the tail, tie seven oblong pieces of pink silk along a piece of thread, then stitch to the bottom point of the kite.

Russian canvaswork dolls

Russian canvaswork dolls

For both dolls you will need:
Persian wool in the following
quantities and colours:
5 skeins red; 4 skeins yellow;
4 skeins green; 2 skeins blue;
4 skeins orange; 1 skein black;
1 skein white; 1 skein pink; 1 skein
fuchsia; 1 skein navy; 1 skein flesh.
70cm (27½in) single mesh canvas,
18 threads to 2.5cm (1in),
70cm (27½in) wide.
25cm (9¾in) unbleached calico
[cotton material] for inner lining,
90cm (35in) wide.
Foam chips for stuffing.
Waterproof felt tip pen or water
proof Indian ink.
Tracing paper.
Tapestry needle.

The inspiration for these two dolls in canvaswork comes from the traditional nesting dolls of Russia. They are simply shaped and easy to make. Each doll is worked in a variety of stitches in the bold clear colours, typical of the character of most peasant art.

Tracing the large doll

From the pattern given trace one half of the front. Fold the tracing paper where the centre line is indicated and trace the reverse side. Open out the paper and strengthen the lines of the now completed front with black felt-tip pen.

Make a similar tracing of the back and one of the oval base.

Cut two pieces of canvas measuring 30.5cm × 23cm (12in × 9in) and one measuring 15cm × 20cm (6in × 8in). Fold one of the larger pieces of canvas in half lengthways and place the crease centrally over the tracing. With waterproof felt pen or waterproof India ink trace the design through onto the canvas. To prevent fraying and the embroidery wool becoming rubbed, turn down and sew, or tape the raw edges of the canvas. Trace the back of the doll onto the second large piece of canvas and the base onto the small piece of canvas.

To embroider the large doll

Using two strands of Persian wool in the needle, work the stitches as indicated by the key on the trace pattern. Begin with the face, hands and bow then fill in the borders of the dress and headscarf [kerchief]. The white straight stitches on the headscarf [kerchief] are simply worked on top of the tent stitch. For the rest of the headscarf [kerchief] work the ribbed spiders first and then fill in the background with upright cross-stitch.

Making up [finishing] the large doll

Block the three pieces of canvas. Trim each one leaving a 1.3cm (½in) seam allowance all round. Turn the seam allowance to the wrong side and tack close to the edge. Clip curves where necessary. Hold edge between fingers and crease. With wrong sides together loosely tack the back and front sections together.

Starting with the headscarf [kerchief] cut two lengths of matching double wool. Lay one length along the outside edge and with the other work overcasting stitches to couch it down, at the same time neatly joining both edges together. With matching wool join remaining side seams together in the same way.

For the inner bag cut calico [cotton material] to the same size as the three canvas pieces, plus 1.3cm (½in) seam allowance. With right sides together, tack and machine the front to the back.

Stitch key
A. Upright cross stitch (over two threads)
B. Cross stitch
C. Tent stitch
D. Upright gobelin (over three canvas threads)
E. Upright gobelin (over two canvas threads)
F. Slanting gobelin
G. Split gobelin
H. Rice stitch (for small doll work in single wool)
I. Ribbed spider
J. Hungarian variation
K. Straight stitch
L. Old Florentine border
M. Back stitch (for small doll work in single wool)
N. Overcasting seams with couched thread

Opposite: The finished dolls – alive with bold, clear colours worked in a variety of stitches.

Trace patterns

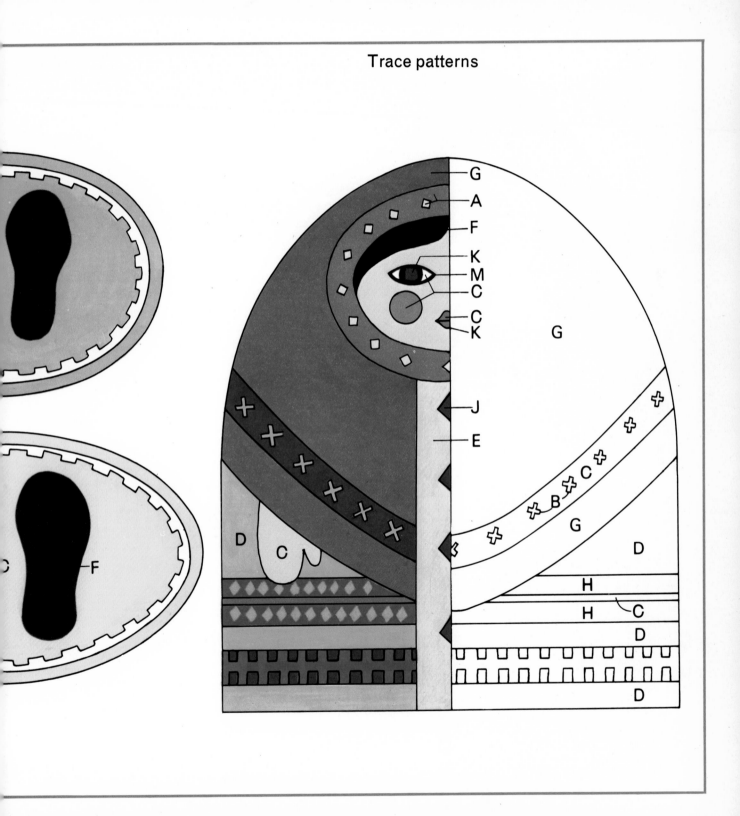

35

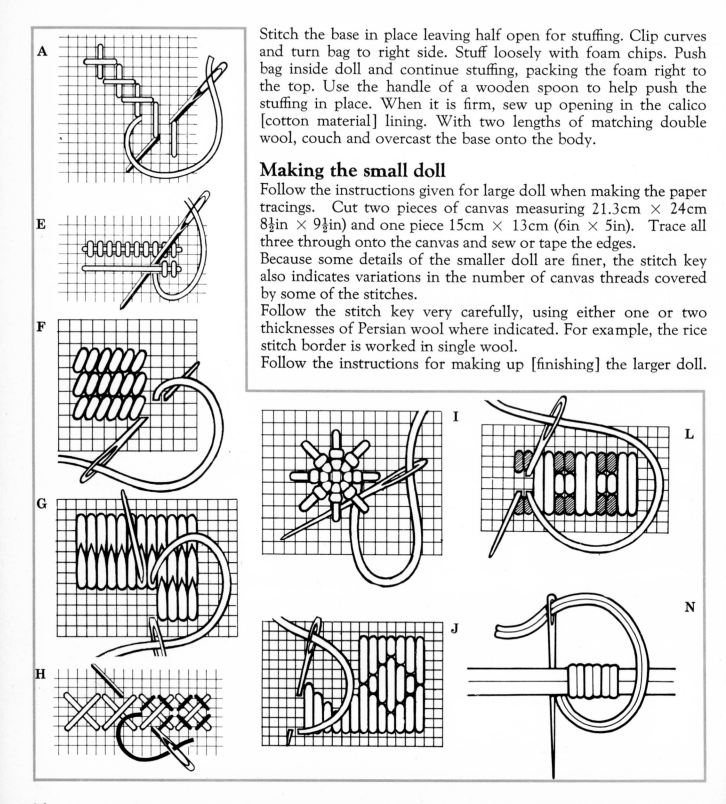

Stitch the base in place leaving half open for stuffing. Clip curves and turn bag to right side. Stuff loosely with foam chips. Push bag inside doll and continue stuffing, packing the foam right to the top. Use the handle of a wooden spoon to help push the stuffing in place. When it is firm, sew up opening in the calico [cotton material] lining. With two lengths of matching double wool, couch and overcast the base onto the body.

Making the small doll

Follow the instructions given for large doll when making the paper tracings. Cut two pieces of canvas measuring 21.3cm × 24cm 8½in × 9½in) and one piece 15cm × 13cm (6in × 5in). Trace all three through onto the canvas and sew or tape the edges.

Because some details of the smaller doll are finer, the stitch key also indicates variations in the number of canvas threads covered by some of the stitches.

Follow the stitch key very carefully, using either one or two thicknesses of Persian wool where indicated. For example, the rice stitch border is worked in single wool.

Follow the instructions for making up [finishing] the larger doll.

Traditional
dolls

Corn dollies

Dolls have always been with us; from the simple figures primitive man shaped in clay to encourage the gods to smile on him, to the elaborately dressed and carefully sculpted fashion dolls of the seventeenth and eighteenth centuries.

Corn dollies are a part of the traditional harvest festivals of England and served as symbols of fertility which were preserved from one harvest to the next. A dolly was usually made with straw from the last sheaf to be gathered. Advances in agriculture have meant that grain is now grown much shorter than it used to be, but since the revival of interest in the craft, long and hollow stemmed varieties are being cultivated specially to make dollies. Alternatively, you can use art straws if you have difficulty obtaining the real thing.

To learn the techniques of this fascinating country craft begin by making an appealing straw angel.

Preparing the straw

Oat and rye straws are specified in the instructions, but wheat straw, which is more easily obtainable, can be substituted. The straw must be specially prepared, or 'tempered', so that it becomes pliable and easy to work. This is done by dampening the straw so that it will bend easily without splitting, but is not soggy.

Cut the straw above the first joint and below the ear as shown in the diagram. Put the cut straw into enough water to cover it completely, then leave it to soak for 10 minutes. Remove the straw from the water and wrap in a damp towel or cloth and leave it for 2 to 3 hours.

While you are working, keep all the straw not actually in use wrapped in the damp cloth to prevent it drying out. Any straw that is left over from a single project should be dried completely in warm air or in a cool oven. It can then be stored in a dry place and tempered again when you wish to use it.

Joining the straw

A single straw may often be too short to complete some of the

Opposite: A collection of dolls and decorations, involving basically very simple techniques.

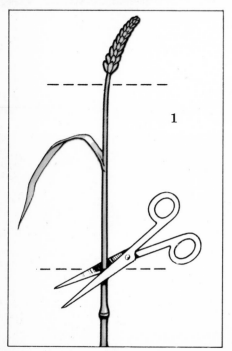

plaits [braids]. If so, join two straws by inserting a slant-cut tip into a straight-cut end as shown in the diagram. The join should be made under a fold in the plait [braid] where it cannot be seen.

To make the angel

To make the body, roll the stiff paper into a cylinder 18cm (7in) long and 2cm (¾in) across. Glue into position.

Take enough of the prepared oat straws to completely cover the outside of the tube, making sure to have an odd number. Cut them into 23cm (9in) lengths and carefully slit them down one side. Open the straws out flat.

Taking each straw in turn, glue 2.5cm (1in) of the dull side of the straw inside one end of the tube. Bend the rest of the straw over the edge as shown in the diagram, and press closely against the tube. Continue until the outside of the tube is completely covered, with an odd number of straws.

Take a narrow straw, as long as possible, slit it open and weave it round the tube, over one straw and under the next, until the tube is completely enclosed.

When weaving is complete, tuck the loose ends of the 23cm (9in) strips inside the tube and glue down.

The head is formed from a Four Plait [Braid] 13cm (5in) long. To work the plait [braid], take four straws and, working on a firm flat surface, lay them out as shown in the diagram. Take straw A over C to lie beside B. Then bring B down over D into the space left by A. Turn the work a quarter circle clockwise. Repeat the two part manoeuvre and turn again. Continue in this way until the plait [braid] is the required length. Always fold the plaits [braids] closely to make a sharp concertina-like edge. Join the ends of the plait [braid] and glue them just inside the cylinder.

The halo is made from a Six Plait [Braid] 18cm (7in) long. Take six of the longest oat straws and lay them out as illustrated. Fold D over to lie between A and F; then take A over to lie between C and E; E crosses to lie between D and B; B crosses to lie between

1

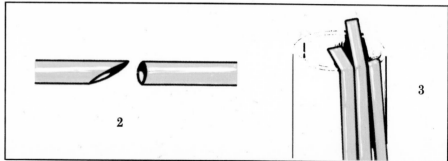

2

3

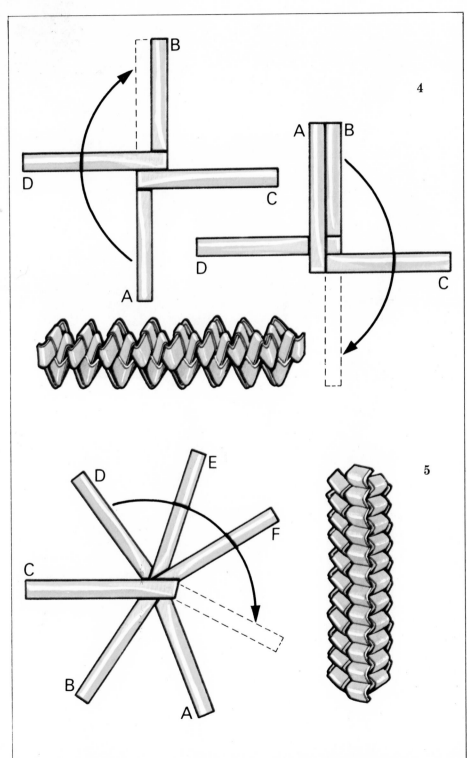

4

5

1. Cutting the straw.
2. Joining two straws.
3. The body: gluing the slit straws over the tube.
4. The head: making a Four Plait [Braid].
5. The halo: making a Six Plait [Braid].

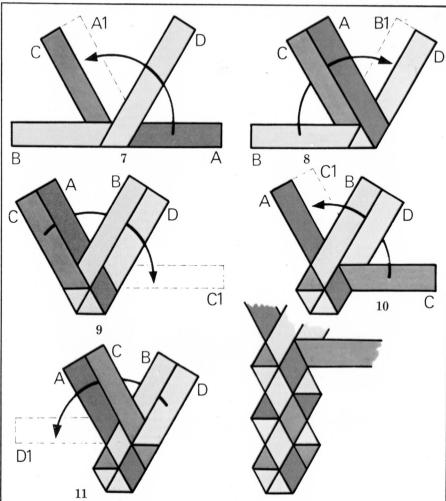

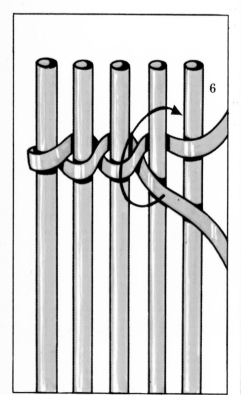

6. *Pairing the straws to form the wings.*

7-11. *The arms: making a Zwemmer Plait [Braid].*

A and F; F crosses to lie between E and C; C crosses to lie between B and D. Continue folding D, A, E, B, F and C until plait [braid] is the required length. Fix the halo to the outside of the cylinder behind the head. If you find it difficult to understand this plait [braid], practise first with labelled strips of paper.

The arms are formed from a 23cm (9in) Zwemmer Plait [Braid]. Following the diagrams take two long oat straws and cross CD over the centre of BA. Then take A over D to lie alongside C (fig.7). Take B under C and over A to lie alongside D (fig.8). Take C under A and B and over D (fig.9). Take C under D and over B to lie alongside A (fig.10). Take D under B and C and over A (fig.11).

The straws will now form the same shape as in fig.2. Continue with the plait [braid], working stages 2, 3, 4 and 5 as shown until

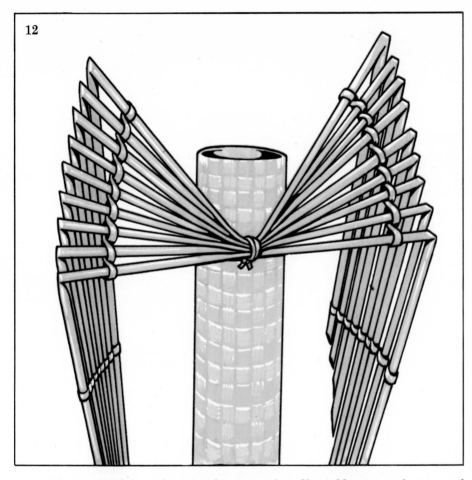

12

12. The wings: back view.

it is the required length. Lay the arm plait [braid] across the top of the cylinder in front of the head and stitch or glue into position. To make the wings you must use an odd number of rye straws (nine were used for the angel shown), each straw 46cm (18in) long. Tie them tightly in the centre so that they fan out around the bottom straight straw. Hold them in position with a row of pairing 5cm (2in) on either side of the centre. To work pairing, follow the diagram. Fold all the straws on a line running from 9cm to 6.5cm (3½in to 2½in) away from the centre. Pair across the bottom of the wing, about 11.5cm (4½in) from the top fold and then trim the ends to a point.

If you have trouble getting the wings to stay in position, re-damp them, putting them upside down in a container of suitable size. Let them dry in the right position. Pin the wings to the body, beneath the halo.

Be sure to dry the angel thoroughly, under the plaits [braids] and in the folds, before putting it away. Keep it in a dry place.

Poupard doll

Poupard doll

You will need:
One 4cm (1½in) diameter wooden ball for the head.
1 piece of 6mm (¼in) dowel rod 25.5cm (10in) long.
Scraps of double knitting wool for hair.
Scraps of pink wool for the hands.
Chenille wire (pipe cleaner) about 24cm (9½in) long for the arms.
A piece of calico [cotton material] 15cm × 11.5cm (6in × 4½in) for the body covering.
Small pill box about 4cm (1½in) deep and 2.5cm (1in) in diameter.
A little rice.
Woodworking glue and 6mm (¼in) bit and hand drill.

Opposite: Two completed dolls – simple and unusual.

The first primitive example of the poupard doll (French for 'doll without legs') was a simple plaything – just a wooden ball head fixed to a stick and wrapped in swaddling clothes to represent a baby doll. The toy enjoyed a revival in the 19th century, when it was elaborated; heads were made of wax and the doll was richly dressed. Noise-making features, such as whistles, squeakers or musical boxes or mechanisms such as a handle for turning the head were frequently added. The modern interpretations here have rattles and tinkling bells. If intended for a younger child it would be advisable to omit the bells and wire arms and ensure that colours for the features are non-toxic. It would be a simple matter to go back to the first principles and dress the doll in washable fabric.

Assembling the doll

Drill a 6mm (¼in) diameter hole in the wooden ball 1.3cm (½in) deep and glue the dowel rod into place (fig.1).
Using enamel paint or the felt pens paint the features either following the features suggested in fig.2 or designing your own. Spread glue on the back of the head and starting from the centre, coil the double knitting wool around the head. The hair style can be elaborated by plaiting [braiding] some additional lengths of wool, twisting to form a bun shape and gluing it to the back of the head as shown in fig.3.
Make a small slit in the middle of the piece of calico [cotton material] just large enough to insert the dowel rod. Slip the material on to the dowel rod with the short sides across the shoulders and the long ends to the back and front. Push the fabric up to the head.
To form the arms take the chenille wire and, working from the centre, twist it around the dowel rod just under the material. This will help to keep the material in place (fig.4). Shape the arms and bind [tie] the ends of the chenille wire with a little pink wool, then loop the ends of the bound [tied] chenille back and bind [tie] them to the arms to form the hands. Glue the arms into

You will need:
25.5cm × 7.5cm (10in × 3in) of
broderie anglaise [eyelet] or lace
7.5cm (3in) wide.
Tracing paper for patterns.
15cm × 5cm (6in × 2in) of calico
[cotton material] for the first
underskirt.
20cm × 35cm (8in × 14in) silky
fabric for the blouse and second
underskirt.
115cm (1$\frac{1}{4}$yds) of 1cm ($\frac{3}{8}$in) narrow
lace for trimming blouse and
bonnet or mob cap.
30cm × 15cm (12in × 6in) velvet
or corduroy for the skirt.
90cm (1yd) of 6mm ($\frac{1}{4}$in) velvet
ribbon.
45cm (17$\frac{3}{4}$in) of 6mm ($\frac{1}{4}$in) nylon.
ribbon.
90cm (35in) of fine braid.
About 18cm × 15cm (7in × 6in)
muslin for the bonnet or 12.5cm ×
13cm × 13cm (5in × 5in) square of
cotton for mob cap.
5 bells, (optional as these are not
recommended if the doll is to be
handled by very small children).

place on the dowel rod.
Make a hole in the centre of the pill box lid and also in the base just large enough to insert the dowel rod. Slide the lid and then the box up the dowel rod, put some rice into the box and glue on the lid. Glue the box to the chenille wire at the top of the rod.
Fold the material down on either side of the box and stitch firmly (fig.5).

Dressing the doll

Take 6mm ($\frac{1}{4}$in) turnings throughout.
For the underskirt, work a row of gathering stitches (fig.6a) along top edge of the broderie anglaise [eyelet] or lace and gather up to fit one long edge of the calico [cotton material]. With right sides facing pin and stitch together.
Work a row of gathering stitches along the top of the calico [cotton material] leaving a long thread for finishing.
With right sides facing stitch the centre back seam.
Draw up the gathering at the waist and stitch firmly to body of doll (fig.6b).
The blouse is cut full length to form a second underskirt.

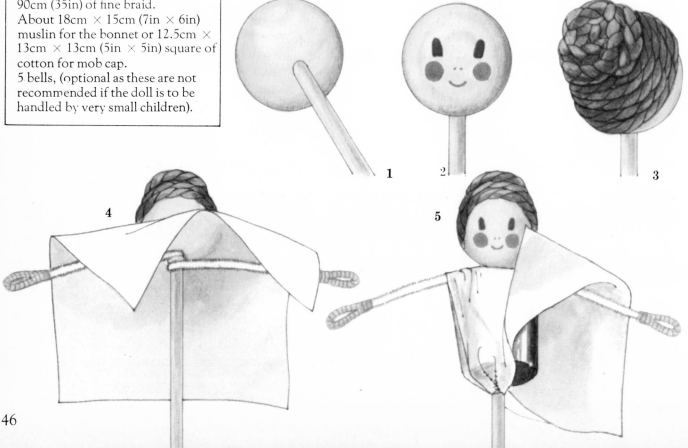

1   2   3

4   5

First cut out a paper pattern using the trace pattern given.
Fold the silky fabric in half to measure 20cm × 18cm (8in × 7in).
Place the pattern with the shoulder edges on the fold and pin into
place. Cut out. Cut an opening in the back at the neck edge large
enough to insert the doll's head.
Stitch 6mm ($\frac{1}{4}$in) hems at the wrist and hem edges.
With right sides together tack and stitch the side and sleeve seams.

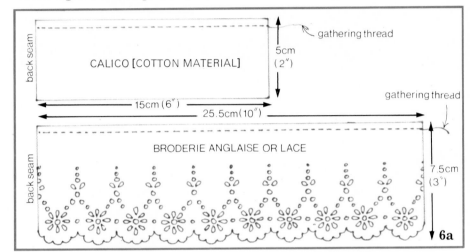

gathering thread

back seam

CALICO [COTTON MATERIAL]

5cm
(2")

15cm (6")

25.5cm (10")

gathering thread

back seam

BRODERIE ANGLAISE OR LACE

7.5cm
(3")

6a

1. The dowel rod glued in place.
2. You can use a felt tip pen to
draw the features.
3. The hair style can be as
elaborate as you wish.
4. How to form the arms.
5. Where to stitch down the calico
[cotton material].
6a. Making the underskirt.
6b. Stitching the underskirt to
the doll.
7. Trim the neck with lace.
8. The finished doll.

6b

7

8

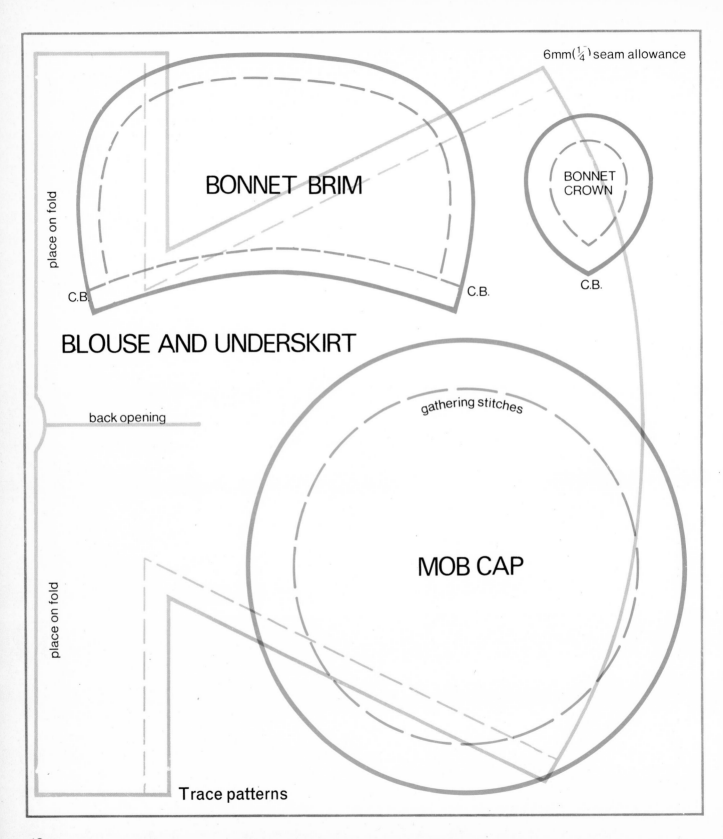

BONNET BRIM

BONNET
CROWN

C.B.

C.B.

C.B.

place on fold

BLOUSE AND UNDERSKIRT

back opening

6mm($\frac{1}{4}$") seam allowance

gathering stitches

MOB CAP

place on fold

Trace patterns

48

Turn to right side. Trim sleeves and hem with lace.

Place the garment over the doll's head and slip stitch the back opening together turning in the raw edges. Trim the neck edge with lace.

Run a gathering thread around the sleeves at the wrists and draw up to fit (fig.7).

Cut the nylon ribbon in half and tie one piece around the arms at the shoulders, tie into bows at the top of the shoulders and stitch into place with tiny invisible stitches.

To make the overskirt, place the two short ends of the velvet together with right sides facing and stitch to form the centre back seam. (If the fabric you have chosen is stiff or thick, less width will be required in the skirt.)

Turn up and stitch the hem.

Turn the skirt to the right side and work a row of gathering stitches along the top, leaving a long thread for finishing. Place the skirt on to the doll, pull up the gathering thread to fit and stitch firmly into place at the waist.

Cut five 13cm (5in) lengths of velvet ribbon and five 13cm (5in) lengths of braid. Sew a small bell to the end of each length of braid and stitch on to the overskirt at the waist alternating with the lengths of velvet ribbon.

Cover the ends of the velvet and braid with a strip of velvet to neaten [finish] and form a waistband. Pull the ribbon tightly covering all the raw edges and stitch firmly into place (fig.8).

Trace bonnet brim and crown from trace pattern given.

Fold the muslin in half to make an oblong 18cm × 7.5cm (7in × 3in) of double fabric, place the brim and crown pattern on to the muslin, pin and cut out.

Turn in a 6mm ($\frac{1}{4}$in) hem around the long curved edge of each brim piece. With wrong sides facing pin together, and at the same time insert and sandwich a 23cm (9in) length of lace trimming between the two brim pieces. Top stitch the layers together with small running stitches.

Starting at centre back stitch the brim to the crown easing any fullness. Cover the raw edges with a double row of lace around the crown.

Place the bonnet on the doll's head. Stitch the remaining piece of braid over the bonnet to form ties (fig.9).

Alternatively, you can make a mob cap for the doll's headdress. Trace the mob cap pattern and cut out in cotton. Stitch a small hem around the outer edge and trim with narrow lace. Work a row of gathers 1.3cm ($\frac{1}{2}$in) away from the edge. Pull up to fit the doll's head and fasten off securely.

9

9. *The finished bonnet.*

Polystyrene dolls' heads

It is possible, and may be easier, to substitute high-density polystyrene balls for the wooden balls used to make the Poupard doll and the Pedlar doll in this section.

Decide on the type of face to be painted and make a working drawing following fig.10 for correct proportions. Support the ball on an orange stick and paint it with an appropriate colour emulsion base coat. When the base coat is completely dry, lightly mark out the features in pencil, then paint them on using a fine paintbrush and appropriate colours of poster paint or gouache. Leave to dry thoroughly.

Warning: polystyrene is an inflammable material and should be kept away from naked flames.

Polystyrene dolls' heads

You will need:
High-density polystyrene balls of a suitable size for intended doll.
Orange stick.
Water-based paints; emulsion paint in flesh tone and poster colours or gouache for features.
Pencil.
Paintbrushes.
PVA adhesive [Duco cement].
Wool for hair (optional).

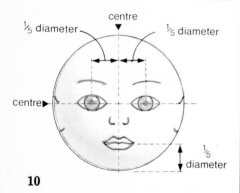

10

Right: A collection of alternative heads for poupard dolls.
10. The proportions of a doll's face.

Pedlar doll

The pedlar doll selling her assorted wares is a charming Victorian idea which would delight children of today just as much. The doll itself is simple to make while the contents of the tray are ingeniously put together from a whole variety of ordinary household objects.

To make the pedlar doll's body

Drill a hole about 2cm ($\frac{3}{4}$in) deep in the wooden ball to fit the dowel then drill a hole in the wood block to fit the dowel. When it is pushed into the ball and the block, there should be about 23cm (9in) of the length showing (fig.1). Do not glue the dowel permanently into the holes until the doll is finished.

To fashion the head, darken the wooden ball a little with brown shoe polish rubbed well in. Trace the face from the trace pattern given. Placing the dowel hole at the bottom, imagine a line half way up the ball but do not mark it in any way. Rub black pencil over the back of the tracing and, positioning the eyes on a level with the halfway line, transfer the features by going over the traced lines with a pencil. Mark the eyes and nose dots boldly with a fine black felt pen and the mouth with the red felt pen outlined with black. Lightly touch in the cheeks with lipstick, then coat the whole head with a matt varnish or a woodseal.

Wind the brass wire once round a pencil to shape the spectacles and fix to the face with a spot of glue.

For the hair, cut fifteen 53.5cm (21in) lengths of grey double knitting wool and, laying the strands side by side, back stitch across the centre with brown cotton. Glue the stitched parting to the centre front of the head, then take the strands to the centre back and tie them together. Apply adhesive to the under side of the hair to hold it in place, but do not arrange it in a bun yet. The rest of the head is covered by the bonnet.

Trace the hand shape from the trace pattern and cut it out in thin cardboard four times. For each arm lay three pipe cleaners side by side and glue a pair of hands into one end, sandwiching the pipe cleaners between the layers (fig.2).

Pedlar doll

You will need:
Doll
7.5cm (3in) diameter wooden ball.
27cm (10$\frac{1}{2}$in) 1.3cm ($\frac{1}{2}$in) diameter dowel rod.
2.5cm (1in) thick piece of wood 7.5cm × 10cm (3in × 4in).
Packet of pipe cleaners.
Small piece of thin cardboard.
Tube of plastic wood in colour to match face.
Red and black fine felt tip pens, pink lipstick.
Matt varnish or wood sealer.
Grey double knitting wool.
Rubber based adhesive.
Pliable wire.
Brass wire.
Hand drill and 1.3cm ($\frac{1}{2}$in) bit.

Doll's clothes
Small piece cream coloured chiffon or other fine fabric.
23cm (9in) square black felt.
Thin cardboard.
70cm (27$\frac{1}{2}$in) of 1.3cm ($\frac{1}{2}$in) wide white lace.
Four small pearl beads for buttons.
Piece of buckram 42cm × 16.5cm (16$\frac{1}{2}$in × 6$\frac{1}{2}$in).
Piece tweed 53.5cm × 19.3cm (21in × 7$\frac{1}{2}$in) with selvedge along one long side.
Piece of fine woollen fabric 39.5cm × 24cm (15$\frac{1}{2}$in × 9$\frac{1}{2}$in) cut on the bias if possible, and small piece extra for collar.
23cm (9in) square white handkerchief.

Cover the hands with plastic wood, pressed onto the cardboard as though it were putty. It may be easier to apply it in layers. Curve the hands round naturally and mark in the divisions of the fingers and the thumbs with a pointed instrument. Smooth the plastic wood as much as possible and sandpaper it when dry if necessary. Twist the pipe cleaners together and twist each set of ends together so that the hands are now 20cm (8in) apart (fig.3). Twist two more pipe cleaners round the whole length of the arms.

If they are still too flexible, bind them with pliable wire. Press the dowel into the head and, about 2.5cm (1in) away from the point where it emerges, cut a deep nick all the way round.

Bind the arms to the back of the dowel with wire in the nick, so that the binding will not slip down (fig.4).

Making the doll's clothes

First make the bonnet. Using the trace pattern for the brim shape, cut two brims from the black felt. Glue one of the brims onto thin cardboard. For the crown cut a piece of felt 10cm × 23cm (4in × 9in). Fold in two across the width and cut away the shaded parts shown in fig.5.

1-6. The principal stages in making the doll.
Opposite: The finished doll and tray.

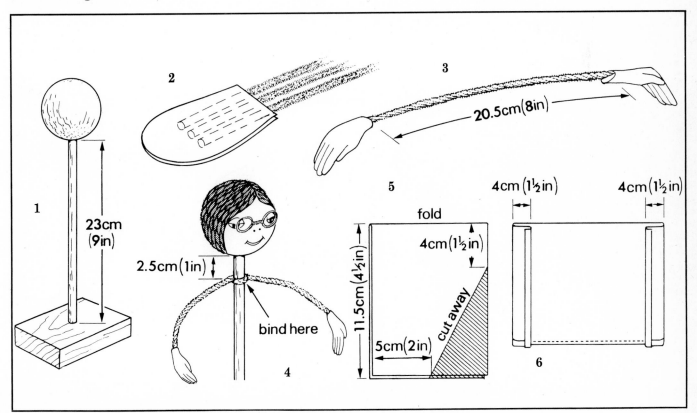

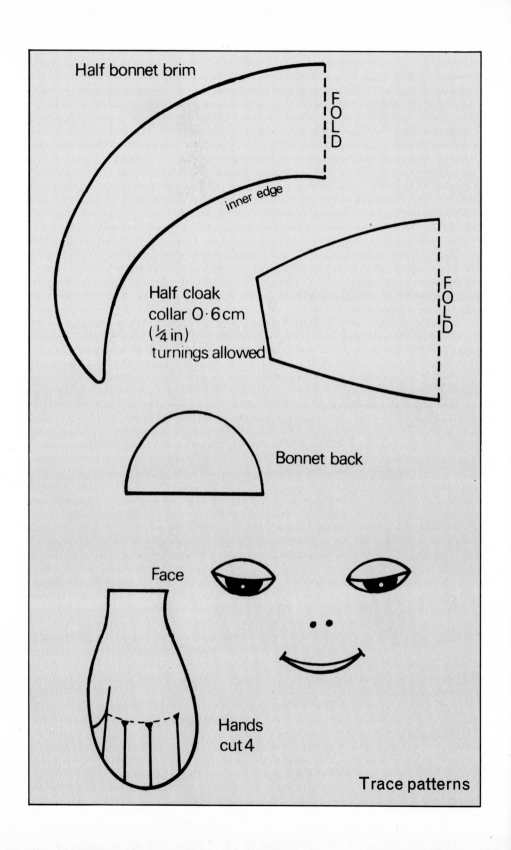

Half bonnet brim

FOLD

inner edge

Half cloak
collar 0·6 cm
(¼ in)
turnings allowed

FOLD

Bonnet back

Face

Hands
cut 4

Trace patterns

Sew the two brims together with the card in between them, then run a gathering thread along the straight edges of the crown and draw up to fit the inner curve of the brim. Oversew [overcast] in place. Run a gathering thread along the long curved edge of the crown and draw up as much as possible. Fit the bonnet onto the doll's head and oversew [overcast] the bonnet back in position. Cut a 38cm (15in) piece of white lace, gather it to at the inside of the brim and catch in place. Glue the bonnet lightly on the head, curl round the remainder of the hair and stitch it into a bun at the back. Glue it down to overlap the bonnet slightly.

Cut a 6mm ($\frac{1}{4}$in) wide strip of felt approximately 10cm (4in) long and make a bow from a separate strip. Sew the bow to the centre of the strip, then stitch the strip to each side of the bonnet so that it rests under the doll's chin.

Using cream coloured fabric for the blouse sleeves, cut a piece 25.5cm × 10cm (10in × 4in) and join the long sides with a very narrow seam for 9cm ($3\frac{1}{2}$in) from each short end, leaving a 7.5cm (3in) gap in the middle. Turn to the right side and slip one of the doll's hands through the gap, then bend the other arm and slip the other hand through. Leave the surplus material in the middle at the back of the doll. Gather the sleeves at the wrist and trim with tiny bands of bias-cut fabric or lace for cuffs.

For the bodice cut two pieces of cream fabric each 7.5cm × 10cm (3in × 4in) and join for 5cm (2in) along each longer side. Turn to the right side. Slip onto the doll and tuck in the remaining raw edges round the armholes. Bring up the top edges and stitch them together for 2cm ($\frac{3}{4}$in) for shoulders, then gather the remainder of front and back for the neck. It will be easier to remove the doll's head while completing the blouse.

Cut a 15cm (6in) piece of lace and gather along one long edge to fit the neck. Stitch in position and catch together at the back.

Sew three or four pearl beads to the centre front for buttons.

Now make the petticoat. Overlap the short edges of the buckram and stitch together. Run a string gathering thread along one long edge. Remove the doll's stand, dampen the buckram thoroughly and draw up to fit the dowel. Position about 7.5cm (3in) below the head.

Shape the rest of the buckram into a bell, flatter at the front, replace the stand and leave the doll in a warm place for the petticoat to dry stiff again.

The skirt is slightly longer than the petticoat and is made as follows. Join the short edges of the tweed and turn the work to the right side, then run a gathering thread along the raw long edge. Slip the skirt over the buckram and draw up the gathering thread. Stitch the skirt in position. If necessary the skirt and petticoat may be kept in position from inside by slipping a circle of card over the dowel and gluing it in place just below the waist.

Make the apron from the 23cm (9in) square handkerchief. Cut a piece 23cm × 15cm (9in × 6in). Gather one long raw edge to about 9cm (3½in) and stitch to the skirt.

Finally, make the cloak. Press a 6mm (¼in) hem to the wrong side of the woollen fabric on one long and two short sides and stitch it down by hand with running stitch. Turn 4cm (1½in) of each short edge to the right side of the cloak (fig.6). Gather up all of the top edge to measure 9cm (3½in).

Cut two collars on the cross from the trace pattern and join them on two short and one long sides with a 6mm (¼in) seam. Turn to the right side. With right sides facing pin the raw edges of collar and cloak together and join with a 6mm (¼in) seam. Press the collar up. Turn in the seam allowance on the inside of the collar and hem down over the raw edge of the cloak. Arrange the cloak over the doll's shoulders and catch the collar together with a short length of fine chain, cord or narrow ribbon as shown in the illustration. Tack the sides of the cloak lightly to the skirt.

The tray and contents

To make the tray, cut a piece of thick cardboard 13cm × 6.5cm (5in × 2½in) and four 1.3cm (½in) wide strips of cardboard to glue round the sides. Cut two 10cm (4in) lengths of brown cord and glue them at the outside corners of each short end to form a loop, then glue 1.3cm (½in) wide upholstery braid all round the outside of the tray. Paint the whole tray dark brown and fasten a double length of cord through the loops at both ends, adjusting it to a length to tie at the back of the doll's neck.

The contents of the tray are made as follows:

Card of buttons Glue tiny beads to rectangles of coloured cardboard.

Knitting needles and hank of wool The needles are sharpened matchsticks or cocktail sticks with beads or lumps of sealing wax on the end; for the hank of wool, wind darning wool a few times round the fingers, twist the loop and fold in half.

Pictures Glue postage stamps on thin cardboard and edge with gold braid. Glue loops of thin cord at the back to hang.

Doll Cut a 5cm (2in) length of pipe cleaner and fold in half with a looped end. Pad this with cotton wool for the head and wind pink wool closely round the doubled end and the two protruding lengths. Cut a 2cm (¾in) length of pipe cleaner for the arms, wind with wool and include the body so that the arms are secured just below the head. Embroider the hair in yellow wool French knots, and paint or embroider the face. Dress the doll in a scrap of felt and add tiny pieces of black felt sewn round the tips of the legs for shoes.

Scarf Cast 10 stitches onto No.14 [00] needles with 3 ply wool and knit about 15cm (6in) in garter stitch. Cast [bind] off and add a fringe to both ends.

Shell ornament Glue a suitable shell for a holder to an inverted limpet, and glue inside it a smaller shell mounted on a length of pipe cleaner, a fragment of another longer shape, a pearl bead and a bit of dried seaweed.

Shell picture Stick a suitable picture, perhaps from a postage stamp, to an oval of cardboard and surround it with tiny shells or

Below: A few of the things worth including on the tray.

pearl beads. Add a cardboard support to the back.

Necklaces Thread small beads and add pendants of larger beads.

Paper flowers Cut pipe cleaners into three for the stalks. Wind them with green tissue. Cut lengths of pink tissue about 2.5cm × 10cm (1in × 4in) and fold in half lengthways. Apply adhesive to the unfolded long edge and wind round one end of the stalk. Tie the bunch of roses together.

Candlestick with candle Use the top from a washing up liquid container, cutting off its lower part where it fits into the bottle. Bore a hole in the top with a heated skewer and fit in a birthday cake candle.

Fan Cut short lengths from collar stiffeners for the struts and glue them together in an open fan shape. When dry, glue lace to the top and trim.

Right and far right: These articles are typical of what Victorian pedlars would have carried.

Hand mirror Cut the mirror shape from cardboard, cover with felt and add a large, flat silver sequin to one side. For a hair brush, prepare as for the mirror but add fur fabric for bristles.

Toasting fork This is made from brass wire.

Salt and pepper pots These are the ends of felt tip pen caps with holes painted on the top.

Lollipops Glue two tiddlywink discs together over the end of a matchstick and cover with cellophane. Make several in different colours and put in a stand.

Scarves Fold scraps of coloured fabric and glue onto the tray.

Pink ball This is a tiny pompon of wool.

Other items which can easily be made include pincushions, picture books, a rolling pin. Odd bits from jewellery or doll's house items can also be added.

Victorian doll

Right: This beautiful Victorian doll owes much of its success to the careful choice of matching fabrics and attention to detail.

Here are complete patterns and instructions for making the body of a Victorian style doll. The completed body can be attached to several kinds of heads which you can either make and paint yourself or which can be purchased, painted or unpainted.

Whatever kind of head is used, it must have not only a neck, but some kind of breastplate or shoulder piece. Otherwise the head will not sit well on the body and will not be stable.

A cast resin, clay or papier mâché head usually has a breastplate with holes drilled in it. The plate is placed over the top of the body and is stitched in place with large firm stitches, using a double thread.

A head made of wood is usually solid, in which case it is inserted into the top edge of the body and firmly glued to the fabric.

If you are painting the head yourself, it is far easier to paint it before attaching it to the body. Some heads have cast hair, such as on the doll's head shown here, which should also be painted at this stage.

If you are adding a hair or wool wig, do not glue it on until the head has been attached to the body and the doll is dressed and entirely finished, since constant fitting of clothes will spoil the hair-style.

It is advisable to decide on the kind of head you are going to use before making up the body (instructions for making a papier mâché head are included in this section) and to make or purchase it accordingly.

The length of the body shown here is four and a half times the height of the head and neck. The body pattern given here is for a body about 48cm (19in) tall, which suits a head and neck about 11.5cm (4½in) high. Use these measurements as a rough guide to check that the body pattern is in correct proportion to the head you have selected. You may find that you have to reduce or enlarge the body pattern accordingly.

The doll's clothes are not sewn directly on to the body, but are made so that the doll can be dressed and undressed, thus enhancing its value as a toy.

The finished doll will not only be an original and exciting toy for your children, but also an object of beauty in itself.

Making the doll's body

It is advisable to use a soft fabric to make the body as this will give a flexible life-like effect. Cotton stockinet [Jersey material] is ideal, but you could use a piece of worn sheet. Cloth which is stiff or contains dressing produces thin stiff limbs, because it does not stretch when stuffed.

Top: A hand-painted papier mache head.
Above: A solid wooden head with real hair.

61

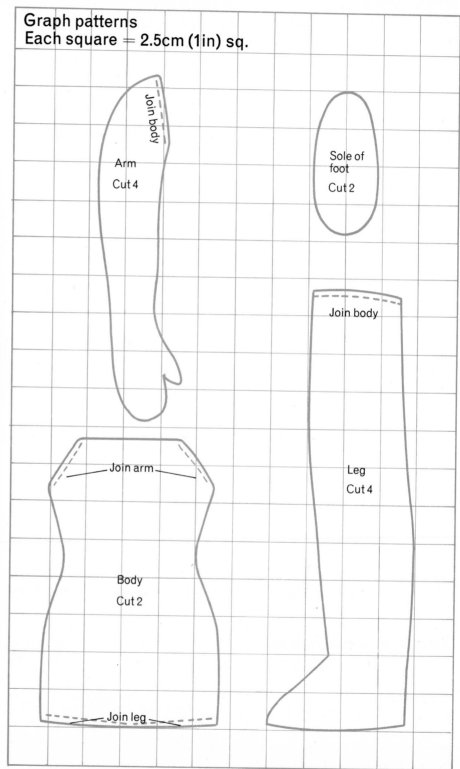

Graph patterns
Each square = 2.5cm (1in) sq.

Join body

Arm
Cut 4

Sole of
foot
Cut 2

Join body

Join arm

Leg
Cut 4

Body
Cut 2

Join leg

Top: An unpainted cast resin head.
Above: A papier mache head
and breast plate.

62

Dip the fabric in a tea bath, using one tea bag to 1 litre (2 pints) of boiling water to obtain a delicate flesh tint.

Make paper patterns from the graph and cut out all the body pieces in the dyed fabric, allowing an extra 6mm ($\frac{1}{4}$in) all round for seams.

With right sides facing, machine stitch round the edges of the legs, leaving the top and feet edges open. Insert the soles in the feet, with right sides facing and narrow end to heel, and machine stitch in place. Turn right side out. With right sides facing, machine stitch round the edges of the arms and trunk, leaving the top edges open. Turn right side out.

Stuff all five pieces from the open top ends. Fill them firmly, putting in small amounts of stuffing at a time. Push the stuffing down with the blunt end of a knitting needle. Turn in the raw top edges of the limbs and overcast them together.

If you are using a head with a breastplate, close the neck edge of the body as for the limbs. If you are using a solid head which is to be glued to the inside of the body, neaten [finish] the neck edge by turning in 6mm ($\frac{1}{4}$in) all round and sewing down neatly, and leave open.

Make a large straight stitch at the front and back of the knees and elbows, using a double thread and taking it right through both layers of fabric and the stuffing. This simulates joints and gives the limbs flexibility. Work running stitches on the front of the hands to indicate fingers and thumbs.

To attach the limbs to the body, join the hand sewn edges at the tops of the limbs to the relevant parts of the body as indicated by the dotted lines on the graph patterns and sew in place.

The body is now ready to be attached to the head.

Making a papier mache doll's head

The basic head shape is made using strips of paper, shaped layer upon layer round a mould. The features (nose, ears, hair-style) are modelled on this basic head shape with paper pulp and secured with more strips of paper to make a smooth surface.

The mould and stand

The mould consists of a cloth bag which is filled with cat box granules [kitty litter] and secured to a modelling stand which is a wooden post fixed on to a wooden block. The granules [litter] absorb the moisture from the papier mâché, helping it to dry easily. The stand makes modelling easier since it provides a steady base on which to shape the papier mâché.

To make the stand drill a hole through the centre of the wooden

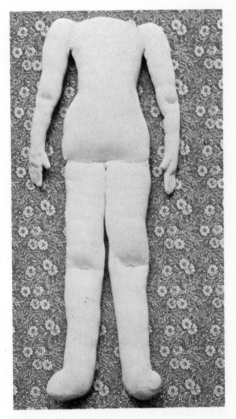

Above: A finished doll's body ready for attaching to a painted head. The doll should be dressed before attaching the wig.

block with the 2cm ($\frac{3}{4}$in) flat bit. Spread glue on one end of the dowel and inside the hole, and hammer the dowel into the hole, to the depth of the wooden block (fig.1). Alternatively, glue the dowel directly on to the block and screw it in place from underneath.

Cut a cross in the centre of the cardboard square and push the dowel rod up through the cut. This will serve as the base on which to form the breastplate.

Make the head mould using the trace pattern provided. Use it to cut three pieces of old sheeting or similar fabric. Seam along the dotted lines on the pattern, sewing the pieces together firmly with strong thread (fig.2). (It is preferable to machine stitch the pieces.) Leave the neck edge open. Clip curves and turn inside out.

Pack the bag with cat box granules [litter], to about 2cm ($\frac{3}{4}$in) from the neck edge of the bag. Hold the stand upside down and push the dowel into the bag, to a depth of about 7.5cm (3in), or so that the mould does not wobble on its stand. Bring the cardboard up to meet it.

Wind strong thread round the neck of the bag and the dowel post just above the filling, and knot securely. Turn the stand and mould upright (fig.3). Bend the cardboard so that it is slightly rounded. Cover the entire mould with a single sheet of newspaper, crush it close to the mould and secure with sticky tape at the base of the neck. This sheet of newspaper is the base to which the paper strips are stuck, and stops the strips sticking to the mould.

Modelling the head

Tear enough newspaper into small strips to cover the mould with at least eight layers.

Dip the strips, one by one, in the wallpaper paste solution and apply to the mould. Apply at least eight layers of paper strips. Using the nail, poke several holes along the front and back bottom edges of the breastplate.

Make up the paper pulp in a bucket by soaking the paper in water for several hours. Then squeeze out the water until the paper is quite pulpy. Then add pulp to the glue using a little less than 0.25 litre ($\frac{1}{2}$ pint) of wallpaper paste solution for one head, mixing carefully with a wooden spoon. You will know when enough pulp has been added to make a firm consistency because, when you squeeze out the excess paste from the pulp, it should bind together as a lump.

Mould the features and hairstyle on the basic head shape with paper pulp when the last layer of paper strips is still wet. Mark the positions of the nose, chin, eyes and ears very lightly with a

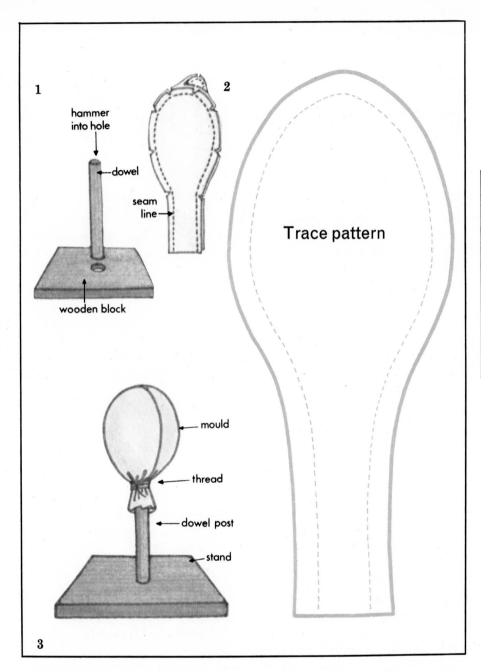

1

hammer
into hole

dowel

seam
line

wooden block

2

Trace pattern

3

mould

thread

dowel post

stand

1. The modelling stand.
2. The sewing mould.
3. The filled mould fixed to the
stand.

cocktail stick or fork.
When the features are formed and while the paper pulp is still
wet, apply another layer of paper strips to secure the features to
the layers of paper strips beneath it. Leave the head on the modelling stand to dry for a day or two, until the surface has a uniformly
pale grey colour and feels dry to the touch.

Carefully turn the head and stand upside down and gently ease out the rod by twisting it carefully. Remove the stand, turn the head right side up so that the granules [litter] fall out of the mould. Pull out the fabric mould and keep it for re-use; it should come away easily.

If the inside of the head is not thoroughly dry, you can put it in an oven at the lowest possible heat and with the door open. Check the head frequently and remove it from the oven as soon as it is completely dry. This may take a few hours.

Painting the head

Cast resin, papier mâché and wooden heads are all painted in the same way. Paint the entire head with white emulsion paint as a base on which to work.

Paint skin, features and hair – if doll has cast hair – using acrylic paint which is fast drying. Mix coloured and white acrylic paints to obtain pale delicate shades and dilute with a little water or acrylic medium. It is also possible to use water colours mixed with white emulsion to obtain the desired colours.

When the paint is dry, you can give the head a coat of non-shiny varnish to make the paint permanent, but this is an optional refinement. Leave varnish to dry.

Polish the head with transparent furniture polish for a translucent effect.

Making a wig

Although dolls' wigs can be purchased, they are usually expensive. You can make the dolls' 'hair' yourself from an old wig. Most wigs are made up by machining hair together into a long, very narrow strip or strips stitched onto a net foundation. Unpick a strip of hair from the net foundation of the wig (see fig.4).

Measure right round the doll's hair-line and cut a strip of wig 6mm ($\frac{1}{4}$in) shorter than this length. Glue it to the head, starting 3mm ($\frac{1}{8}$in) away from the centre top of the hairline, wrapping it round to the base of the head and bringing it back up to the other temple, 3mm ($\frac{1}{8}$in) from the centre top of the hairline, thus leaving a 6mm ($\frac{1}{4}$in) gap at the centre of the crown.

Repeat this process using shorter and shorter strips of the wig and progressing towards the back of the head until you have covered the sides and back of the head (fig.5). Fill the gap along the centre of the head with four straight strips of hair cut to the required length. This will give the effect of a centre parting. The hair can then be trimmed and set.

Apply setting lotion to the hair with absorbent cotton and set the hair with hair clips. When the hair is dry, remove the clips and brush hair into the required style. Curls can be catch-stitched in place for permanence.

Hair can also be made from wool. Make a skein of wool 5cm (2in) thick and 35cm (14in) long, and work a row of back stitches across its centre to indicate a parting. Glue this to the head, matching the parting to the centre of the head and pull wool down on either side. Put a dab of glue where the doll's ears should be and glue the wool in a bunch to each ear. This will leave a bald patch at the back (fig.6).

Twirl the wool up towards the back of the head into a bun to cover the bald patch and catch stitch in place (see fig.6).

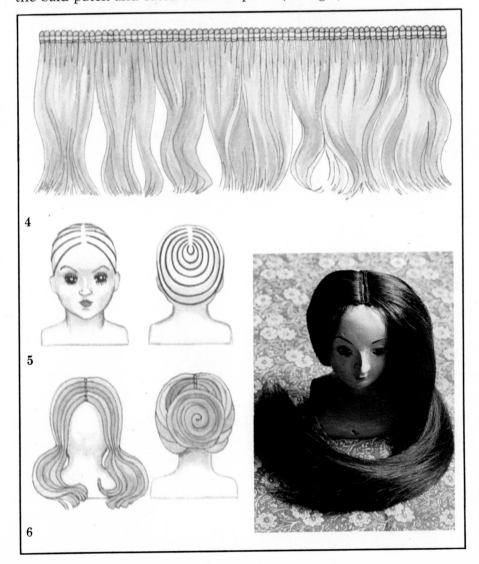

4

5

6

4. A strip of hair, unpicked from the net foundation of an old wig.
5. The positioning of strips of hair.
6. A bun covers the bald patch at the back.

67

Victorian
doll's clothes

Having made the Victorian-style doll, you will now want to dress her in period fashion. The graph patterns are for a complete wardrobe, including underwear, boots and bonnet.

These clothes can be made very cheaply, particularly if you already have scraps of suitable fabrics and trimmings. Be sure to use tiny beads and fine lace for decoration, as too heavy a trim will spoil the proportions.

If you have had to adapt the body pattern to suit the doll's head, make sure that you alter the clothes patterns likewise. The patterns are designed to fit the body perfectly, but you should check the fit of the clothes on the doll as you work, as you would if making your own clothes. As the clothes are all tight fitting, it is particularly important to obtain the correct fit.

You can adapt the patterns given here and use your imagination to create an entirely different wardrobe for your doll.

Make paper patterns for all the clothes using the graph patterns given. Allow an extra 6mm (¼in) for seams all round.

Boots

Cut boots, soles and heels out of fabric. No seam allowance is needed on soles and heels. With right sides facing, machine stitch back seams. Turn right side out.

Wrap the boots round the legs and turn in the front edges by 6mm (¼in) so that they meet edge to edge. Sew neatly in place. Glue the soles into position, sticking them to the soles of the doll's feet and the inside edges of the boots. Glue the heels in place. For a firm, neat finish, work running stitch round the outer edges of the soles and heels.

Sew small beads in pairs at approximately 1cm (⅜in) intervals to either side of the front join. Using contrasting embroidery silk, sew cross stitches down the front of the boots so that the point of each cross coincides with a bead, to suggest lacing.

Underwear

Corselet [camisole] Cut out the four pieces for the corselet [camisole] from the fabric.

With right sides facing, stitch the four pieces together at side and back seams.

Neaten [finish] the front edges by turning in 6mm (¼in) and machine stitching.

Fasten the front overlap with press studs [snap fasteners] or hooks and eyes.

Add narrow lace for shoulder straps and trim the front and bottom edges with narrow lace.

Below: A delightful wardrobe for a Victorain doll, typical of the period.

Pantaloons Cut out the two pieces for the pantaloons from the fabric.

With right sides facing, machine stitch the centre seams.

Fold right sides together, so centre front seam lies on centre back seam, and machine stitch the inner leg seams.

Make a hem [casing] at the waist edge and thread elastic through.

Turn right side out. Add lace trim to the leg bottoms.

Petticoat Cut out the four petticoat pieces from the fabric. With right sides facing, machine stitch the four panels together.

Hem the waist edge and thread narrow elastic through.

Sew lace trimming to bottom edge.

Dress

The Victorian style of dress consists of a very tightly fitting bodice with full skirt and sleeves.

Cut out the bodice, sleeves and skirt panels from dress fabric.

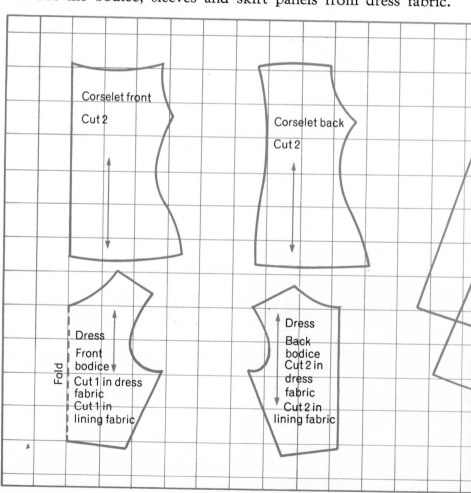

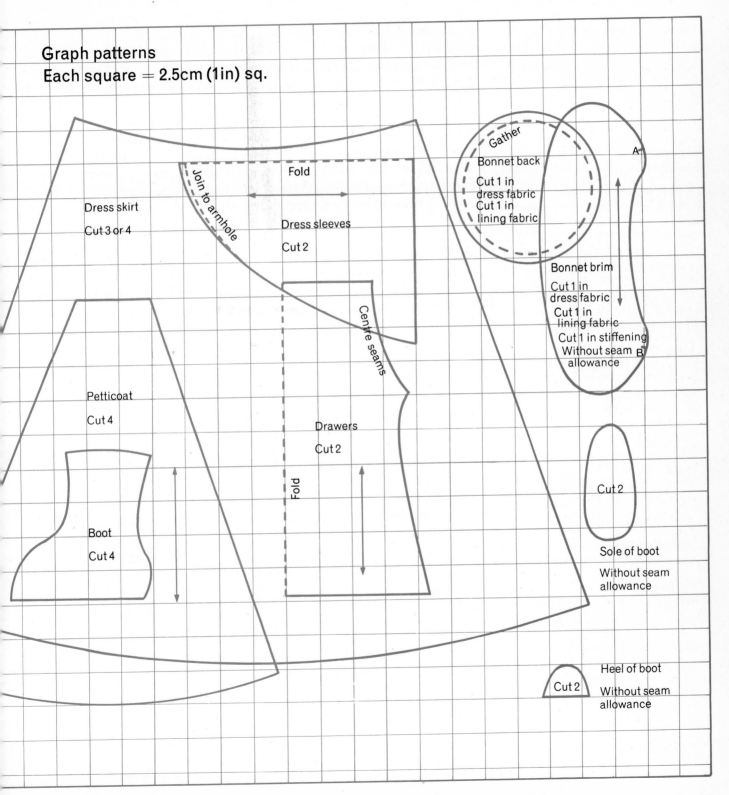

Graph patterns
Each square = 2.5cm (1in) sq.

Dress skirt
Cut 3 or 4

Fold

Join to armhole

Dress sleeves

Cut 2

Gather

Bonnet back

Cut 1 in
dress fabric
Cut 1 in
lining fabric

A

Bonnet brim

Cut 1 in
dress fabric
Cut 1 in
lining fabric
Cut 1 in stiffening
Without seam
allowance

B

Petticoat

Cut 4

Centre seams

Drawers

Cut 2

Fold

Cut 2

Sole of boot

Without seam
allowance

Boot

Cut 4

Heel of boot

Cut 2   Without seam
allowance

Also cut bodice from lining fabric.

With right sides facing, stitch both bodice and lining at side and shoulder seams. Sew lace trimming to bodice.

Place lining to bodice, right sides facing and seams matching, and stitch along back edges and neck edge. Turn right side out and tack lining to bodice round armholes and waist edges.

Fasten back overlap with press studs [snap fasteners] or hooks and eyes. Sew lace trimming to the sleeves as illustrated.

With right sides facing, stitch inner arm seams. Hem the sleeve edges and thread elastic through for a gathered effect.

Sew sleeves to bodice by sewing armhole seams by hand, with right sides facing, and working bodice and lining together as one. Stitch the skirt panels together, right sides facing, leaving open a small section of the top of one seam. This will be the back seam. Turn right side out. Sew lace trimming to skirt near the bottom. Gather the top of the skirt with running stitch, and sew skirt to bodice by hand, with right sides facing and again working bodice and lining together. Make a small hem round the bottom of the skirt.

Bonnet

Cut out a circular back section and a brim for the bonnet from dress fabric and lining. Also cut a brim piece without seam allowance from stiffening.

Place the two brim pieces together, right sides facing, and stitch round the curved ends and longer side leaving the section between points A and B open. Turn right side out and insert stiffening. Place the two back sections together, right sides facing, and stitch round the edge, leaving a gap through which to turn. Turn right side out and slip-stitch opening.

Work gathering stitches with a double thread round the edge of the circular back section, close to the edge. With right sides facing, stitch the top fabric of brim between points A and B to the back section. Turn in the seam allowance on the lining of the brim and slip-stitch in place.

Draw up the gathering threads on the back section so that the bonnet fits the doll's head, and fasten the loose ends. Sew ribbons high up on either side of the inside of the brim. If they are too low, they will pull the brim down when tied under the doll's chin. Sew a lace frill to the back section of the bonnet where it is not attached to the brim and cover the brim with an assortment of lace trimmings to match the dress.

To make ear rosettes, gather up two small lengths of fabric or ribbon to form two flower shapes and sew one to each end of brim.

Dress

1.8m (2yd) of 90cm (35in) wide fine fabric such as muslin [thin cotton] or silk, or 1.4m (1½yd) of 90cm (35in) wide heavy-weight fabric such as tweed for the skirt and bodice.

If you use a fine fabric, cut four skirt panels from the paper pattern. If you use a heavy-weight fabric only cut three panels. This will result in a less full skirt, but the waist would otherwise be too bulky when gathered into the bodice. The quantities given are sufficient to make the matching bonnet.

Matching thread.

Light-weight fabric such as silk or fine cotton to line bodice.

Assorted lace trimming.

4 press studs [snap fasteners] or hooks and eyes.

Narrow elastic for sleeves.

Tiny beads for decoration.

Bonnet

Fabric to match dress – see fabric requirements for dress.

Matching thread.

Fine fabric for lining. A smart co-ordinated effect is obtained by using the same fabric as for the petticoat and pantaloons.

Paper or buckram for stiffening.

Assorted lace trimming to match dress.

Ribbon for tying bonnet under doll's chin.

Miniature
dolls

Bead dolls

Bead dolls are very easy to make, and many different characters can be created depending on your imagination and the variety of beads available. The examples shown here have a bizarre, mysterious character reminiscent of ethnic talismans. The basic construction is the same for each character; the difference is in the colour and type of beads used and the features given.

The head

The head can be made from a polystyrene, Styrofoam or cotton waste ball. First of all a hole is made through the centre of the head – this can be done with a hot pin through polystyrene, or a metal knitting needle through Styrofoam and cotton waste.

A piece of string or wool is then passed through the hole and a knot made at each end. One end of this piece of string is used to hang up the doll and the body is attached to the other end. The head can be covered with suede or felt, which is glued on, or painted a suitable colour.

The features can be made in several different ways. On the Chinese doll (second on the left in the photograph), the head is completely covered with threaded beads wrapped round a Styrofoam ball in a spiral and glued in place. To do this, the beads must be threaded so that the features and hair fall in the right place. Alternatively, the features can be painted on or made from beads attached to the head with pins. If the holes in the beads are too large to be held in place by a pin, a sequin between the pin head and bead will solve this problem.

The hair can be made of plaited [braided] wool, pins and beads or strings of threaded beads (fig.1). The long strings of threaded beads should be tied to a double length of string or wool which is then attached to the head with pins (see fig.1).

The body

The body is attached to a small curtain ring – about 1.3cm ($\frac{1}{2}$in) inside diameter – which is then attached to the head. The beads should be threaded on to strong thread.

The curtain ring is first bound with wool to match the colour of the head, then the body is attached to it. If the body is to be clothed, the clothes can be made out of a long 'curtain' of beads attached all round the ring as on the three dolls on the left in the photograph. This is done by threading lots of strings of beads all the same length and tying them on to the ring. Patterns can be created by threading different coloured beads.

To make arms, legs and a torso, thread two long strings and two shorter strings and attach them to the ring. Then tie the upper

Below: Just four of the many dolls that can be created using different beads and lots of imagination.

half of the two longer strings together to form the torso (fig.2).
If you wish to make the arms and legs bend, thread them on to
fuse [lightweight copper] wire instead of thread.

With the doll on the right in the photograph further embellish-
ments have been added. This is done by stringing beads, attaching
them to a piece of thread and then tying round the 'ankles',
'wrists' and 'waist'. You could make up your own costume for a
doll using the same technique.

When the body is finished it is attached to the piece of string
which was threaded through the head. So that the body will hang
straight, make a criss-cross of threads on the curtain ring and
attach the head to the centre of the criss-cross (fig.3). Be sure to
get the front of the doll facing in the same direction as the face!

*Above: Detail of the head of
one doll.*
*1. The 'hair' can be made from
large beads, plaited [braided]
wool or strings of beads attached
to the head.*
*2. The body, arms and legs
attached to the curtain ring.*
*3. How to attach the curtain ring
to the head.*

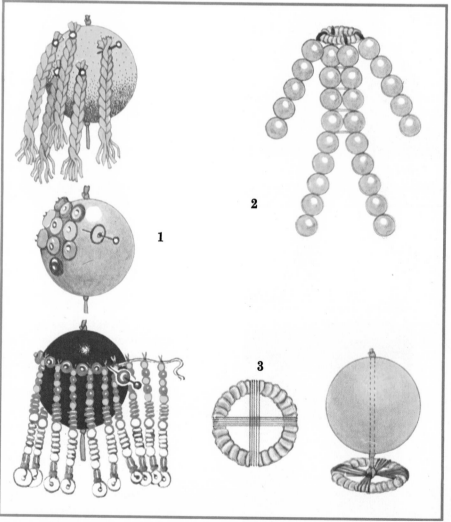

Wooden robot

This very simple, ingenious toy will give a child many hours of pleasure. Using off-cuts of wood and dowel rod it is a very cheap toy to make. Following the basic construction techniques described more unusual off-cuts may be used to construct robots that appear to be really out of this world.

For the doll shown here, select pieces of wood that will give the proportions of the robot, i.e. thicker dowel rod for the legs than for the arms, and for the head a piece of wood at least half the size (or smaller) than that of the body.

To position the arms drill a hole through the block used for the body, slightly larger than the dowel which will pass through it. This will allow the arms to swing freely. Drill holes of the same size through the dowels which will form the arms.

Smooth the blocks of wood with fine sandpaper.

Assemble as illustrated. Glue two pieces of dowel to the bottom of the body for the legs.

Glue on a block of wood for the head. The head is not in the centre but should be placed slightly towards the back of the robot.

This is a very simple toy to make and if left to dry thoroughly will stand up to some rough handling. It can be varied and made more flexible by drilling a hole in the bottom of the head and another one in the trunk, and then by using a piece of dowel for the neck, allowing the head to turn around.

Wooden robot
You will need: Off-cuts of wood and dowel rod of various thicknesses. Hand drill and bits to correspond to dowel rod sizes. Fine-grade sandpaper. Wood glue.

1. The arms are attached to a piece of dowel which passes through the chest.

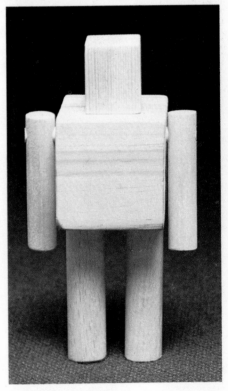

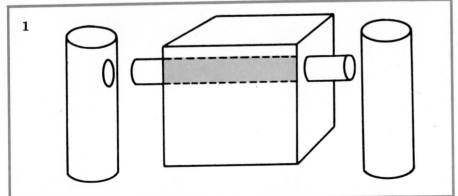

Clothes peg dolls

Some of the very earliest dolls were simply wooden sticks, painted and draped with colourful scraps of cloth. And when the first pegs [clothespins] appeared they soon replaced the sticks as ideal doll shapes, with their ready made 'heads', 'bodies' and 'feet'. We show you here a small collection of delightful dolls made from scraps of fabric and threads. After you see how easy they are to make, wouldn't it be fun to see how many more you can create, using your own ideas?

Below: Although all of these dolls are made from pegs [pins], each one can still be made excitingly different from the next.

Painting the pegs [clothespins]

Choose the most perfectly shaped pegs [clothespins]. Avoid rough splintered surfaces where they would be seen, and such things as uneven legs and heads.

Lightly sandpaper each all over. Give a coat of primer to the head and shoulders and to the toes and body, if they are to be seen. In the case of the ballet dancer, prime all over. Leave to dry and then give two coats of white enamel to each primed part. Use the side of a shoe box to peg [pin] the dolls onto while drying. If the face and toes are to be painted in any other colour, such as the Indian, give two coats of light brown enamel after the primer. Paint in the face next. It is easier to create successful features if they are painted simply as dots and placed symmetrically under the hair parting (fig.1).

Paint pale blue or black eyes, pink cheeks and a red mouth. Leave to dry. Then the shoes of the ballet dancer should be painted in, and again left to dry.

To make the ballet dancer

Cut six small notches into the leg where the laces would cross (fig. 2).

Cut two lengths of pink stranded cotton about 15cm (6in) long and lay the centre of one of them on the shoe line along the inside of the peg [clothespin] (fig.3).

Hold both ends of the cotton; lace into the notches by crossing over and making a knot at the top. Using pinking shears cut out four circles of mauve net 10cm (4in) in diameter. Fold each piece in four and cut across the folded corner to a depth of 1.5cm ($\frac{5}{8}$in). Glue about ten mauve sequins onto each layer of net (fig. 4).

To make a foundation for stitching on the skirt, wind a length of mauve thread a few times around the waistline of the peg [clothespin], knot and cut ends. Take two layers of net together and run a gathering thread around the top. Slip over the peg [pin]; stitch into place. Sew the other two layers of lace in the same way. With a brighter colour of pink thread wind round a bra line.

Cut two small pieces of net 2.5cm (1in) by 1.3cm ($\frac{1}{2}$in), stitch together and shape into a bow. Glue to head.

To make the peasant doll

From a fairly heavy patterned linen cut a rectangle measuring 13cm × 15cm (5in × 6in), preferably with the selvedge to run across the bottom of the dress. With the right sides facing, fold in two and sew side seams. Turn to right side and press seam flat. Turn in neck edge to wrong side and press. With running stitches

---

Clothes peg [clothespin] dolls

You will need:
Clothes pegs [clothespins].
Sandpaper.
Wood primer.
Enamel paints as used in model making in the following colours: black, brown, white, red, blue and yellow.
Turpentine substitute for cleaning brushes.
Two finely pointed hair paint brushes, sizes 1 and 2.
Off-cuts of net, cotton, and silk material, lace edging, broderie anglaise [eyelet], narrow white ribbon, various small pieces of felt and imitation leather, beads and stranded cottons, sequins, linen.
Glue.
Three small dried flowers.
Dried lavender.
Small sharp knife.

1

80

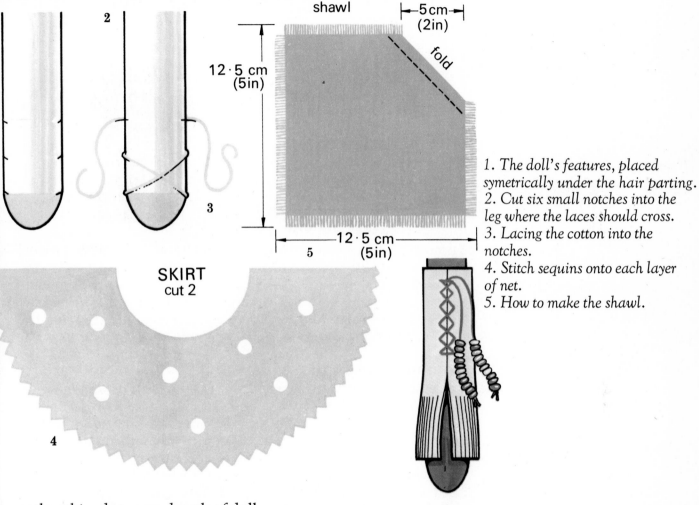

1. *The doll's features, placed symetrically under the hair parting.*
2. *Cut six small notches into the leg where the laces should cross.*
3. *Lacing the cotton into the notches.*
4. *Stitch sequins onto each layer of net.*
5. *How to make the shawl.*

SKIRT
cut 2

gather this edge around neck of doll.
From a contrasting coloured cotton cut a 13cm (5in) square. Cut across one corner to a depth of 5cm (2in) (fig. 5). Turn this edge of the shawl over twice. Put it over the head and fold the sides round the face. Tie in place around neck of peg [clothespin] with a fine thread. Arrange the folds to fall in front and trim bottom edge with pinking shears.

To make the lavender seller
From a fine material such as silk or lawn cut a rectangle measuring 13cm × 15cm (5in × 6in). Fold over and seam down the long sides and across the bottom. Turn inside out, press seams, turn in top edge and sew with running stitches. Fill bag with an egg-cupful of dried lavender. Insert painted peg [clothespin] and pull running stitches to gather fabric round neck.

6. *Finishing off the head.*

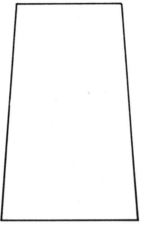

6

Trace pattern

To make the apron cut a square from the broderie anglaise [eyelet] 5cm × 5cm (2in × 2in), sew around three sides and turn inside out and press. Sew a 13cm (5in) length of white 6mm (¼in) wide ribbon along top edge and tie around doll. To make the shawl follow the instructions given for the peasant doll but fraying the bottom edge to about 6mm (¼in).

To make the Indian squaw

Trace off the skirt pattern and lay it on the back of the imitation leather, trace around it twice and cut out two pieces. With red stranded cotton cross stitch the top halves of one side together. Fit the skirt onto the doll and cross stitch the other side, leaving long enough strands to thread on about twelve small beads in red, black, green and white and make a knot. Fasten ties.
Cut twelve lengths of black stranded cotton measuring 9cm (3½in) and glue to back of head. Plait [braid] and tie around bottom with black cotton. Cut a bright pink felt feather and glue to back of head. Group a selection of coloured threads together and glue around head, tie with knot and cut off leaving 1.3cm (½in) ends (fig.6).

To make the bride

Cut one rectangle of broderie anglaise [eyelet] 23cm × 9cm (9in × 3½in) and sew fine lace edging to bottom. Fold and sew long sides together. Press flat. Turn in top edge. Using running stitches gather top edge around the neck. Cut a length of scalloped-edged lace 28cm (11in) long and glue at centre head. Cut the bottom edge of the lace at 30° to sit straight at ground level.
Thread a bouquet of two or three small dried flowers through the eyelets of the broderie anglaise [eyelet].

Pipecleaner dolls

The time required to make a miniature doll is not necessarily in proportion to the size of the doll. A 15cm (6in) doll may take just as long to make as a much larger doll. Many different materials are involved and most of the sewing must be done by hand. Meticulous care and accurate detail are part of the joy of making miniature dolls, however, and much satisfaction is to be gained from creating the right effect.

Trace patterns are given here for clothes for a family of dolls—mother, father, girl, boy and governess. The patterns do not include seam allowances and 6mm ($\frac{1}{4}$in) must be added all round. The dolls vary slightly in height—from approximately 15cm (6in) for the children to 18cm (7in) for the father.

The clothes patterns should only be regarded as a basic guide and each pattern should be checked against the completed body for which it is intended before cutting out to ensure a correct fit.

The dolls are dressed in clothes which were fashionable during the early 1900s; patterns can easily be adapted to suit other household characters or to make clothes of a different period.

By using the same basic pattern shapes, choosing different fabrics and trimmings, altering the skirt lengths and adding a variety of detail, you can create an entire collection of delightful miniature people.

These dolls are extremely cheap to make and dress since they only involve inexpensive materials, all of which are used in small quantities.

The bodies are made from pipecleaners, absorbent cotton, bias binding, pink cotton fabric or felt for the head and scraps of knitting wool for the hair.

The clothes can be made from any scraps of fabric you may already have but it is preferable to use closely woven, non-fraying fabrics which give a neat finish and involve less work. If you use patterned fabrics, try to choose small patterns that are in proportion to the size of the dolls.

Felt is particularly suitable for clothes such as jackets and hats, as well as for trimmings since it does not fray.

Pipecleaner dolls

To make the basic body
You will need:
Three pipecleaners.
Absorbent cotton
Pink bias binding.
Small piece of pink felt or cotton fabric for the head.
Matching thread.

Narrow ribbon and lace are useful for collars, touches of decoration and binding [tying] edges.

To make the basic body

Join the pipecleaners together as shown in fig. 1a. You can adjust arm and leg lengths by making an extra twist or two round the body.

Following fig. 1b, pad pipecleaner 'skeleton' with absorbent cotton and wind sewing thread round it to keep it in place.

Wind pink bias binding round the legs, arms and body in overlapping layers as shown in fig.1b and catch stitch in several places to hold the layers in position, particularly at the ends of the arms.

Make a paper pattern for the head using the trace pattern given and cut out the two head pieces in pink felt or cotton fabric.

With sides facing, sew round the edges, leaving the neck edge open. Trim the seams and turn right side out. Stuff the head with a little absorbent cotton, place over the top of the pipecleaner ends, and continue to stuff until you have obtained a proper head shape (see fig.1b). Catch-stitch the neck edge neatly to the body all round.

The mother

Make the body as described. To emphasize the S-line of the Edwardian dress, pad the bust and seat with extra cotton.

Dress Cut out paper patterns for the skirt, bodice and sleeves from the trace patterns given. Check the length and width against the doll. Lay all the patterns on a double thickness of fabric and cut out. With right sides facing, sew front bodice pieces to back bodice at shoulders and sides. Turn right side out.

Wrap a short piece of broderie anglaise [eyelet] round the neck of the doll to form a high collar. This can be trimmed to 1.3cm ($\frac{1}{2}$in) at the sides and back of the neck, but should be wide enough at the front to make a blouse front under the V-neck. If the trimming is already too narrow for this, sew a piece of white ribbon to the front of the doll's body before putting on the collar. Put the bodice on the doll. Turn in the neck and front edges and sew to doll along the fold line.

Pull the sleeves on to the arms, turn under the armhole edges and stitch to bodice. Sew one or two layers of narrow lace trimming on to cover this stitching line.

To make the skirt, sew the back seam, right sides facing. Turn right side out. Put the skirt on the doll, turn in at the waist and sew to the bodice, starting at the front and gathering at the back to obtain a bustle effect.

Turn up and sew the skirt hem and the sleeve edges (unless you

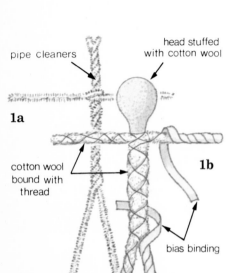

pipe cleaners

head stuffed with cotton wool

1a

cotton wool bound with thread

1b

bias binding

1a, b. Making the basic doll's body.

Opposite: An entire family of pipecleaner dolls.

84

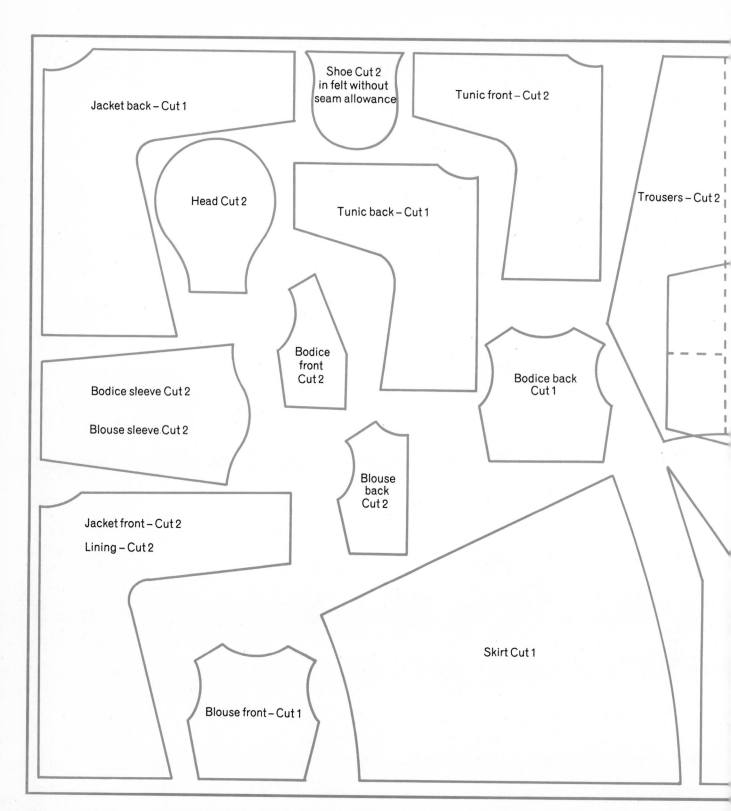

Jacket back – Cut 1

Shoe Cut 2
in felt without
seam allowance

Tunic front – Cut 2

Head Cut 2

Tunic back – Cut 1

Trousers – Cut 2

Bodice
front
Cut 2

Bodice sleeve Cut 2

Blouse sleeve Cut 2

Bodice back
Cut 1

Blouse
back
Cut 2

Jacket front – Cut 2

Lining – Cut 2

Skirt Cut 1

Blouse front – Cut 1

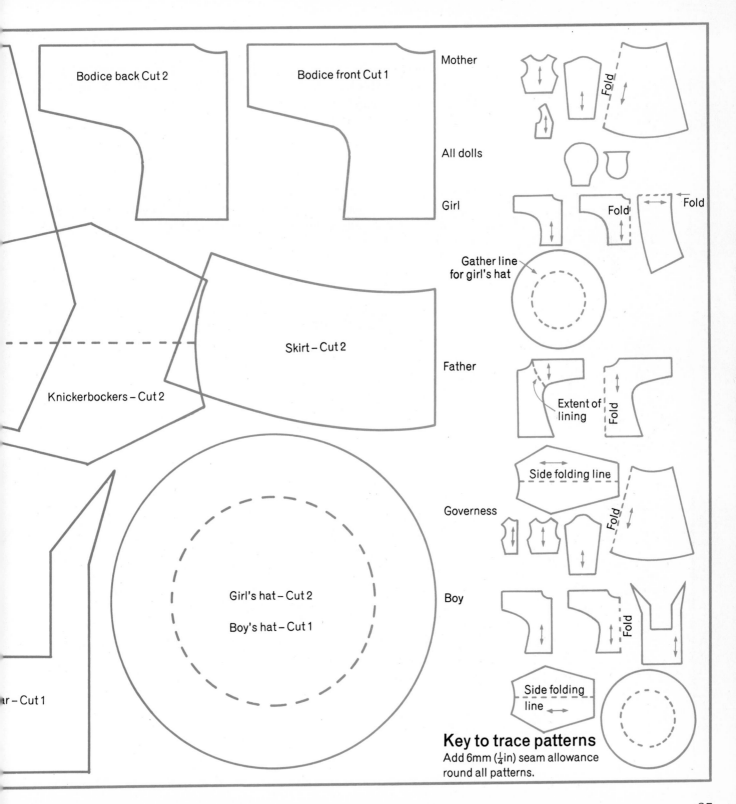

Bodice back Cut 2

Bodice front Cut 1

Skirt – Cut 2

Knickerbockers – Cut 2

Gather line
for girl's hat

Girl's hat – Cut 2

Boy's hat – Cut 1

ar – Cut 1

Mother

All dolls

Girl

Father

Fold

Extent of
lining

Fold

Governess

Side folding line

Fold

Boy

Fold

Side folding
line

Key to trace patterns
Add 6mm ($\frac{1}{4}$in) seam allowance
round all patterns.

have managed to cut these edges against a selvedge or have used non-fraying fabric).

To make the train, use a piece of ribbon or lace about 10cm (4in) square. Taper the ribbon or lace to 5cm (2in) at the top and 10cm (4in) at the bottom by folding in the sides by the required amount. Sew to the back of the skirt at the waist and sew down with a couple of stitches on either side of the train. A waist [half-] petticoat could also be made using the skirt pattern. Add lace trimming to the bottom edge for a feminine touch.

Hair Sew wool on to the head, starting at the top and working from the centre parting to the sides. Loop more wool loosely at the sides and finish with a bun on top of the head. Embroider features on face of doll.

Hat Make a frame out of pipecleaners with a 2.5cm (1in) crown and approximately 5.5cm (2¼in) brim (fig. 2). Cover the frame by winding brown ribbon or tape round and round the frame in layers lengthwise and catch-stitch in place at intervals.

Cut out two or three different sizes of coloured felt circles, preferably with pinking shears. Arrange them around the hat in layers, and sew on.

The hat can simply be pinned on to the head, or, if young children will be playing with the doll, it should be sewn permanently in place.

The governess

Make body and the skirt as for mother and also the blouse but omit V-neck and make opening at back.

Put the skirt and blouse on the doll, sew up back overlap of blouse, turn in sleeve edges and hem and sew. Trim the sleeve edges with ribbon to indicate cuffs.

Sew on a strip of felt at the waist for a belt and embroider a buckle. Make the collar by wrapping a piece of white ribbon or binding round the doll's neck and sewing down at the back. Cut out a small felt bow and sew to the collar front.

Hair Sew knitting wool on to the head, working from front to back, and finishing with a neat bun at the centre back. Embroider features.

Make a pince-nez by bending fuse [copper] wire to required shape and sewing in place between the eyes. Attach one side of the frame to a piece of black wool or very narrow cord and tuck the other end into the belt.

The father

Make the body as before, but slightly taller than that of the mother.

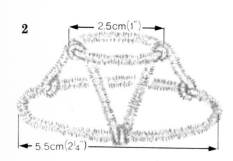

2

2.5cm(1")

5.5cm(2¼")

2. The pipecleaner frame for the hat.

Make paper patterns for trousers, jacket and sleeveless lining for front of jacket using trace patterns given. Check for size against the doll's body.

Lay all the patterns on a double thickness of fabric and cut out.

Trousers With right sides facing, join centre front and centre back seams.

Lay trousers so that front and back seams lie on top of each other, and join inner leg seams. Trim seams and turn right side out.

Put the trousers on the doll and sew to body at the waist, gathering in any surplus width. Turn in trouser hems and sew.

Jacket With right sides facing, sew front pieces to back piece at sides and shoulders. Turn right side out. Pin lining to front of jacket on each side, with right sides facing, and sew along shoulders and front edges. Trim seams and turn lining to inside of jacket. Make back collar by binding edge with matching ribbon or jacket fabric. Press flat.

Make the shirt collar with a small length of white ribbon or bias binding turned in at edges. Sew round the doll's neck, leaving a small gap at the front. Make a shirt front by sewing a piece of white ribbon to the front of the doll's body. For a cravat, tie a knot in black ribbon and sew in position on shirt neck.

Put the jacket on the doll. If the jacket is too wide at the back, it can be taken in by making a tuck at each shoulder.

Turn in the sleeve hems and sew. Turn back the lapels and catch stitch in place. Details, such as felt or bead buttons, pockets and a breast pocket with handerchief, may all be added if desired.

Hair Sew knitting wool to head, starting at centre front and working to sides and back. Begin with long stitches and build up with shorter ones. Embroider features, whiskers and moustache.

The girl

Make doll's body as before, but about 2.5cm (1in) shorter than that of the mother.

Make paper patterns for the bodice, skirt and hat using trace patterns given and check against the doll for size. Lay them on double thickness of fabric and cut out.

Dress With right sides facing, sew front bodice to back sections at sides and shoulders. Turn right side out. Turn in and sew neck edge. Put the bodice on the doll, turn in edges of back opening and join by overlapping and sewing down.

Sew side seams of the skirt, right sides facing. Turn right side out. Pin and sew skirt to bodice, taking large pleats as you go. Turn up and sew sleeve edges and hem.

If the pleats stick out, sew down each pleat.

Trim sleeves and neck with narrow lace and trim waist seam of skirt with narrow ribbon.

Hair Sew long lengths of knitting wool from centre parting to sides and back, securing it at ear level. Embroider features.

Hat With right sides facing, join edges of two circular hat pieces, leaving a small gap.

Trim seam and turn right side out through gap. Turn in edges of opening and oversew [overcast] them together. Gather at line shown on trace pattern to fit head. Press edge of brim. Trim gathering line with ribbon. Attach to head as for mother's hat by pinning or sewing in place.

The boy

Make the body as for the girl doll.

Make paper patterns for sailor's outfit using trace patterns given. Check against doll for size. Lay patterns for tunic and trousers on double thickness of fabric (preferably white for tunic and navy-blue for trousers) and cut out.

Lay the patterns for hat and collar on a single thickness of navy-blue fabric and cut out. It is a good idea to make the collar in felt, to avoid turning in the edges. In this case, trim away the 6mm ($\frac{1}{4}$in) seam allowance from the paper pattern.

Knickerbockers Make the trousers as for the father. The only difference is that they reach just below the knees.

Sew the knickerbockers to doll's legs, taking a tuck on the outside of each trouser leg and trim with a strip of blue felt or ribbon.

Tunic Make the tunic as for the girl's bodice, but with the opening at the front.

Trim collar with a thin strip of navy felt or narrow ribbon and trim sleeve edges at wrist with two strips of navy-blue felt or narrow ribbon. Trim collar piece at the back and sides with a strip of white felt stitched in place near the edge.

Fasten collar piece at front by sewing to blouse at the point where the ties cross.

Hat Gather the circle of fabric at the edge so that it fits the head and flatten the crown.

Sew a narrow band of felt round the edge of the opening, and sew this band to the head. Add two small strips of felt at one side of the head. Stitch brim to head in one or two places to keep the crown flat.

Shoes

The shoes for all the dolls are made from felt, using the trace pattern given (no seam allowance is necessary).

Doll's houses

Cloth house

Cloth house

You will need:
1.8m (2yd) of 6mm ($\frac{1}{4}$in) quarter round dowelling. [molding].
46cm (18in) of 13mm ($\frac{1}{2}$in) dowel rod.
Four 23cm (9in) square biscuit or cake [cookie] tins.
3.2m (3$\frac{1}{2}$yd) of 1.5cm ($\frac{5}{8}$in) wide furnishing [upholstery] braid.
2 black beads.
Scraps of adhesive [contact] paper, wrapping paper, felt, velvet etc. for interior decoration.
Small pieces of felt for doorsteps and window boxes.
Black and white soft embroidery cotton.
2 empty thread reels.
Thick cardboard.
Contact adhesive [tape] and fabric glue.
Fine string; fine wire.
Piece of felt 23cm × 69cm (9in × 27in).
57cm (23in) tweed fabric.
57cm (23in) canvas.
57cm (23in) lining fabric.
23cm (9in) fine white net.
23cm (9in) of 5cm (2in) wide black Cluny lace.
1.4m (1$\frac{1}{2}$yd) narrow black lace.
57cm (23in) white guipure lace.
Approximately 24 flower shaped sequins and tiny beads.

Transform four cake [cookie] tins into a pair of elegant Georgian town houses. The front of the houses can be folded back to reveal four floors of rooms, which can be filled with simple furniture ingeniously made from household items.

To make the house front

Draw up the graph pattern onto stiff paper. The dotted lines indicate the position of the balcony and railings. Cut out the twelve windows and the two fan lights over the doors, and pin them in position on the canvas. Tack around the edges of the windows and lightly mark their positions with ballpoint pen. Remove the paper patterns.

Cut a piece of net for each window, allowing an extra 4cm (1$\frac{1}{2}$in) all round, and tack in position over the windows.

Using white thread, work a straight machine stitch around each window, and then work a close satin stitch over this, using a wide setting on the machine. Alternatively, work two more rows of straight stitching close to the first.

Carefully cut away the canvas windows from the back of the net, and darn any accidental snips with invisible thread. Mark the lines dividing the window panes and the fan lights with running stitch, using soft white embroidery cotton, as shown in the illustration. The window boxes on the top storey are formed in the same way, using black embroidery cotton.

Cut six felt strips 2cm ($\frac{3}{4}$in) wide for the window boxes, and either machine or sew neatly in place by hand, leaving the top edges open. Sew the sequins in position around the window boxes and attach a small bead to the centre of each. Alternatively, cut small circles of felt to form the flowers.

Cut the white guipure lace into ten 5cm (2in) strips, and sew in position over the windows to form the window headings [valences]. The doors are cut from felt, and stitched in position on the canvas using a close zigzag stitch. Alternatively, sew them in place neatly by hand.

The door panels are worked by machine using black thread.

Trace and cut out the doorsteps from white felt, and mark the dotted line with straight machine stitching, using black thread. Embroider a circle or horseshoe shape in satin stitch on each door, to form the door knockers, and attach the black beads to form the handles.

Trace off the balcony roof and cut out from felt. Scallop the lower edge, and stitch in place as shown, leaving the scallops free. The markings are in straight machine stitch, using black thread.

The ground floor railings are formed by stitching the narrow black lace in a curve, following the dotted line on the graph. Make

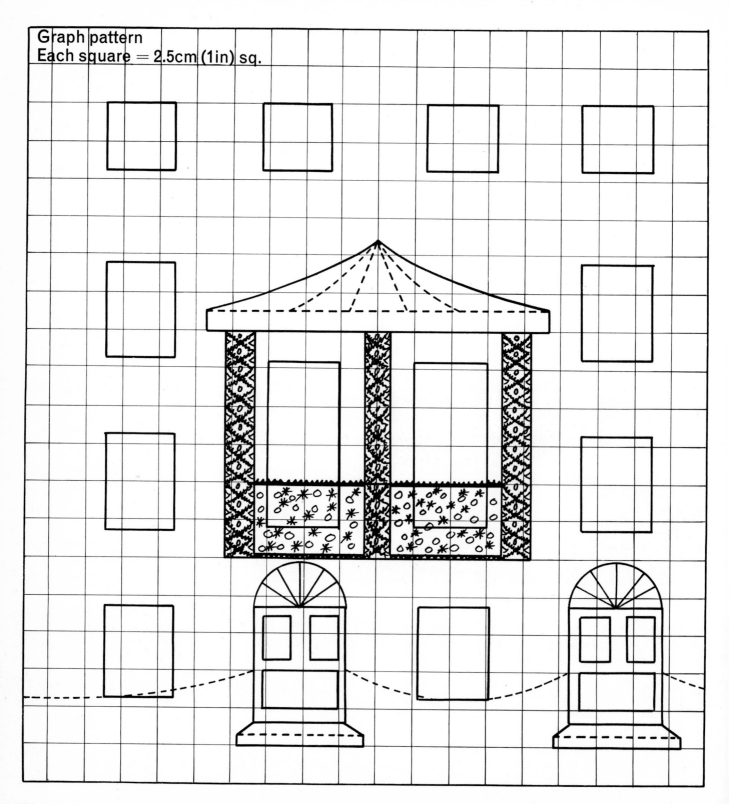

Graph pattern
Each square = 2.5cm (1in) sq.

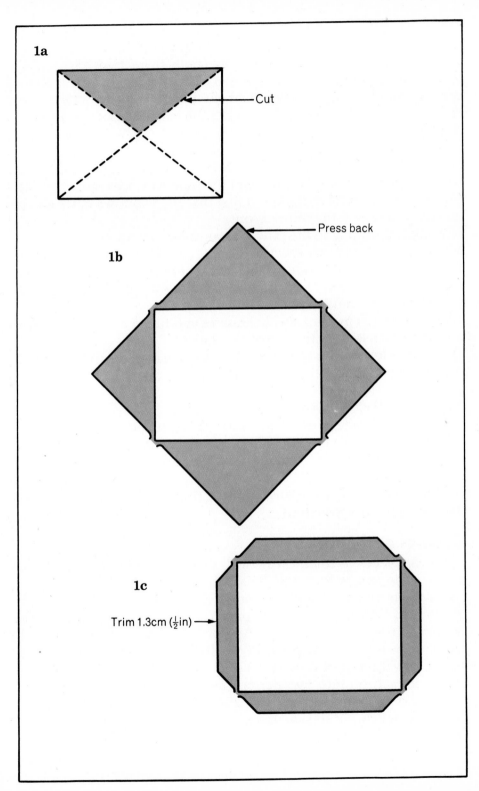

1a

Cut

Press back

1b

1c

Trim 1.3cm ($\frac{1}{2}$in)

1a, b, c. Cutting the lining from behind the windows.

straight railings as shown, either in stem stitch or back stitch, using black embroidery cotton, or work them on the machine.

The three balcony pillars are each made from two 15cm (6in) lengths of narrow black lace, stitched side by side. Sew the straight edges of the lace to the outside of the pillars, and oversew [overcast] the top edges of the pillars under the balcony roof. In between the bases of the pillars stitch two pieces of the wide black lace. Draw up the graph pattern onto the lining fabric.

Draw two diagonal lines across each window and cut (fig. 1a). Press back the triangles (fig. 1b) and trim them off to 1.3cm ($\frac{1}{2}$in) (fig. 1c). Make sure before pressing the lining that the windows correspond exactly to those on the canvas fronts.

Slip stitch the lining to the canvas around each window.

Measure the canvas to exactly 46cm (18in) square, and press the excess fabric at each side to the back. Trim the canvas only to 2.5cm (1in) all round. Trim and turn in the sides of the lining, and slip stitch to the canvas.

Leave about 7.5cm (3in) surplus canvas and lining at the top of the work to attach later to the top of the house.

Turn in the lower edge to the wrong side to make a channel [casing] for the dowel. Stitch in place and insert the dowel.

To make the houses

Decorate the inside of each tin using oddments of wrapping paper, adhesive [contact] paper or fabric, to represent wallpaper remembering that each tin is divided into two rooms by a horizontal partition.

On the front edges of the tins, trim the paper to 1.3cm ($\frac{1}{2}$in), so the edges may be covered later.

Ceilings and floors

Cut eight pieces of thick cardboard, each 23cm (9in) long and the depth of the tins, to form the divisions.

Cut sixteen pieces of quarter round dowel [molding], the depth of the tins. Either paint or glue paper to one side of each piece of cardboard to form the ceilings. Apply fabric glue to three edges of the wrong side of each piece of cardboard, then press four into position at the top of each tin and glue the other four in position to divide each tin into two floors. Paint the dowel [molding], two for each ceiling, and apply contact adhesive to the straight edges. Stick in place on either side under each ceiling to give extra support and to form the coving.

Cut the pieces of fabric to size and glue in place to form the carpets. If desired, the top floor can be divided in two vertically.

To assemble the houses

Glue the sides of the four tins together to form a unit 46cm (18in) square. Tie fine string firmly around the outside of the unit to hold it together and leave it to dry. Leave the string in place when the glue has dried, to give added strength to the unit. Cut two 50cm (20in) lengths of furnishing braid and glue them centrally across the front of the unit, from top to bottom and from side to side, leaving an extra 2.5cm (1in) at each end. Glue braid all round the outside edge of the houses, so that it projects for approximately 6mm ($\frac{1}{4}$in). Attach the house front to the main unit by sticking the upper edge to the top of the tins with plenty of glue. Tie another piece of string tightly around the unit, 1.3cm ($\frac{1}{2}$in) from the front edge, to ensure the front of the house is fixed securely in place.

Roof and outside of houses

Cut two lengths of tweed, each 90cm (35in) long, and the depth of the tins plus 5cm (2in). Join the short edges together, taking a 1.3cm ($\frac{1}{2}$in) seam, and press a 2.5cm (1in) hem along both sides of the long edges.

Apply glue to the sides of the tins, paying special attention to the braided front edges. Press the tweed in place, covering the top, bottom and sides of the tins, so that the raw edges meet at a lower corner. Overlap the ends, trim and sew in place neatly.

Cut a second piece of tweed 48cm (19in) square, and oversew [overcast] it to the back edges of the side coverings, turning in any surplus by approximately 1.3cm ($\frac{1}{2}$in) as you work.

Cut two pieces of cardboard for the roof, each 25.5cm (10in) long, and the depth of the tins plus 1.3cm ($\frac{1}{2}$in).

Cut two pieces of tweed to the same size as the cardboard, plus 1.3cm ($\frac{1}{2}$in) all round. Glue the tweed to the pieces of cardboard, first pressing the extra fabric to the inside.

Apply felt to the other sides of the cardboard, and oversew [overcast] the two fabrics together around the edges.

Sew two short ends of the cardboard pieces together and glue a 6mm ($\frac{1}{4}$in) wide strip of felt to cover the join.

Cut a strip of felt 50cm × 2.5cm (20in × 1in) long. Scallop one long edge and sew it to the covered cardboard so that the scallops hang down.

Take the two empty thread reels and cover them with felt to match the roof. Glue the reels on their sides in the centre of the house tops, one at the front and one at the back.

Glue the centre of the roof on top of the cotton reels and apply adhesive to each short end of the house top. Glue the roof down at each end, and then sew a few extra stitches at each end.

Polystyrene house

Polystyrene house
All textures **You will need:** Expanded polystyrene sheets or tiles. These can be bought in a variety of thicknesses up to 15cm (6in) Liquid detergent. Cream emulsion paint. Poster paints in various colours. Sharp knife such as a scalpel. Three 2.5cm (1in) brushes. Mixing board or heavy cardboard.
Bricks **You will need:** Poster paints in dark red, orange, blue and dark grey. Wax crayon in any colour. Wire engraving tool. Coarse glasspaper and ruler. Polystyrene sheet or tile at least 5cm (2in) thick.
Oak **You will need:** A straight wire engraving tool. Dark grey-brown, blue and pink poster paint. Polystyrene sheet or tile at least 1.3cm (½in) thick.

Making a doll's house

A playhouse or large doll's house can be clad with polystyrene sheets (these should be at least 10cm (4in) thick) and textured to give an authentic and attractive finish.

A doll's house covered in this way will obviously not last long—polystyrene is a rather fragile material—but it will provide a lot of fun for children and will probably survive until they have lost interest in it. It is therefore not worth doing any very fine, detailed texturing if the doll's house is to be subjected to rough treatment.

One way of making the textured doll's house is to completely cover an existing structure with polystyrene which is then textured and painted as described later to simulate bricks, stones and other materials.

Another way, if you have a large strong cardboard box or tea chest for a house, is to give the house a polystyrene front.

Make up front of house as shown (fig. 1). Glue polystyrene sheets with PVA adhesive [Duco cement]. Attach one side of the front to the house with hinges made of wide adhesive tape such as carpet tape, and the other side with a metal hook and eye catch, screwed and glued with PVA adhesive [Duco cement] into polystyrene and the box.

Warning Remember that naked flames should be kept away from polystyrene as it will burn quite easily. If possible, you could obtain polystyrene which has been treated with a flame retardant. Polystyrene is so versatile, adaptable and easy to handle that it can be cut, textured and painted to imitate all kinds of other materials such as wood, stone, brick and metal. These finishes are comparatively easy to achieve with a little practice.

Basic requirements

All textures use variations of the same techniques. They are engraved or cut, then given a base coat of special emulsion mixture followed by highlighting with paint or polishing with metalic powders. For best results carefully study the surface to be simulated before starting work.

Techniques

Engraving The required texture is cut with a knife or carved with an engraving tool into the surface of the polystyrene before painting. Polystyrene engraving tools are made out of wire bent into different shapes and bound on to wooden handles.

Painting To make the base coat, emulsion paint is mixed with the appropriate shade of poster paint to achieve the required colour. A few drops of liquid detergent are added to the mixture. The liquid detergent will make the polystyrene porous.

Dry-brushing When the base coat is dry, the surface is brushed over with a very small amount of paint. A suitable quantity of the required colour is mixed up and a few drops are placed on a piece of card. These drops are picked up with a dry brush and brushed over the surface of the painted polystyrene.

Bricks

Using the sharp knife, cut a sheet or tile of polystyrene for a brick wall of the required size. Mark out the bricks with a wax crayon and ruler.

Heat the engraving tool over a flame and cut away a shallow 'ditch' between the bricks.

Fold a small piece of glasspaper in half and use the folded edge to roughen up the polystyrene to resemble the texture of bricks.

Mix up dark red base coat. Paint the base colour over the bricks making sure that the paint reaches every crevice.

Wait until the base coat is dry, check for white patches and then give a second coat if necessary.

Mix up a small quantity of orange-red paint and then dry-brush bricks.

Add a little blue to orange-red paint and lightly dry-brush again. Add a little cream emulsion to orange-red paint and dry-brush. Paint the courses [ridges] between the bricks grey.

Wood texture

The following method for obtaining an oak finish applies to other wood finishes but the colours and grain texture will vary.

Study the wood before choosing your colours.

Cut the polystyrene to size. Study a piece of real oak and lightly engrave into ridges or make nail holes if required.

Mix up a grey-brown base coat. Mix emulsion paint with grey-brown poster colours and liquid detergent and apply two base coats.

Dry-brush with cream emulsion, then with a blue-cream mixture and finish with a light touch of pink.

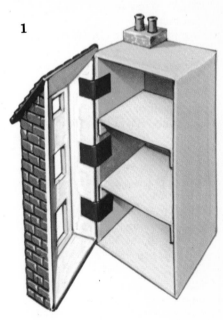

1

Top: This doll's house has been textured with tiles for the roof, bricks for the walls and wood for the door.
1. Attach the front with hinges made of thick adhesive tape.

Wooden house

Wooden house

You will need:
Materials
Two pieces 6mm ($\frac{1}{4}$in) plywood,
30.5cm × 46cm (12in × 18in)
end walls.
Two pieces 6mm ($\frac{1}{4}$in) plywood
35cm × 53.5cm (14in × 21in)
front and back walls.
Two pieces 6mm ($\frac{1}{4}$in) plywood,
20cm × 57cm (8in × 22$\frac{1}{2}$in) –
roof sections.
Two pieces 6mm ($\frac{1}{4}$in) plywood,
28cm × 35cm (11in × 14in)
interior walls.
One piece 6mm ($\frac{1}{4}$in) plywood,
28cm × 53.5cm (11in × 21in)
interior floor.
One piece 1.3cm ($\frac{1}{2}$in) plywood,
46cm × 61cm (18in × 24in) – base.
Offcuts of 6mm ($\frac{1}{4}$in) plywood.
Sheet of clear plastic.
Roll of 6mm ($\frac{1}{4}$in) wide orange
adhesive tape and a similar roll
of yellow tape – obtainable from
office suppliers.
One piano hinge, 25mm × 57cm
(1in × 23in) – for the roof hinge.
Four 1.3cm ($\frac{1}{2}$in) brass hinges and
screws. One hook and eye catch.
One box of 1.3cm ($\frac{1}{2}$in) panel pins.
Two pieces 6mm ($\frac{1}{4}$in) quadrant
beading [corner molding], 35cm
(14in) long. A cross-section of this
beading [molding] looks like a
quarter of a circle.
Enamel paints and suitable
undercoat.
Wood filler and primer.

A doll's house will give you and your children hours of fun. To make this two-storey house requires only the basic techniques of carpentry.

The house, made of plywood, is designed so that there is easy access to the rooms. The front of the house slides out so that child-

ren can play with the furniture inside. The top floor can be reached through the roof which is hinged so that it folds back.

Each floor is divided into three sections consisting of a central hallway with a room on either side. The completed house is 46cm (18in) tall, 30.5cm (12in) deep and 53.5cm (21in) wide.

Each room can be decorated individually and with imagination as you would your own home with either bought or home-made furniture. Working out interior decoration schemes will provide a great deal of pleasure.

Preparation

Buy the plywood cut to the sizes specified. You will have to cut out the smaller sections such as doors and windows yourself (see plan).

The base Take the baseboard and, using a saucer turned upside down, draw an arc in each corner to round the corners. Cut out using a fret [copping] saw or, if you have it, cut with a jig saw attachment for an electric drill. Make sure that each arc is the same size.

The exterior walls Take the pieces of plywood which are to form the end walls of the house and mark out the fall of the roof as shown in the plan. Cut the wood to shape using the tenon [copping] saw.

Mark out the windows according to the measurements given in the plan. On the front and back walls mark out the spaces for the doors and windows, again referring to the plan.

With the drill and the 6mm ($\frac{1}{4}$in) bit, drill holes at each inside corner of the windows. This will enable you to insert the saw blade to cut out the windows. Also cut out the door sections. Cut out the windows on the end pieces, using the same method.

When cutting out the door and window sections do not rush but work carefully. If some of the windows are not square, use a wood file to straighten the edges.

Finish off the surfaces with medium glasspaper. Fig. 1 shows the exterior walls after the windows and doors have been cut and the wood painted.

Interior walls and upper floors The aim here is to make two cross-halving joints on the interior walls and upper floor to enable them to slot into position. The pieces should fit tightly enough not to need gluing.

On each interior wall piece draw the floor level. This should be 18cm (7in) from the bottom of each piece (see plan).

Mark two lines to indicate the slots for the joints on the walls. The lines should be 6mm ($\frac{1}{4}$in) wide and 14cm ($5\frac{1}{2}$in) long. Measure accurately.

You will need (contd.)

White woodworking adhesive and glasspaper – medium and fine grade.
20 screws 6mm ($\frac{1}{4}$in) long.
10 No.4 screws 2.5cm (1in) long.
Tools
Drill with 6mm ($\frac{1}{4}$in) and 3mm ($\frac{1}{8}$in) bits.
Fret saw and tenon saw [copping saw].
6mm ($\frac{1}{4}$in) wide chisel.
Saucer and pencil.
Mallet and small hammer.
Screwdriver, hand plane and coarse file.
One fine paintbrush and a 50mm (2in) wide paintbrush.
Tape measure and carpenter's square.

Opposite: The finished house with the front wall taken away and the roof flapped open.

101

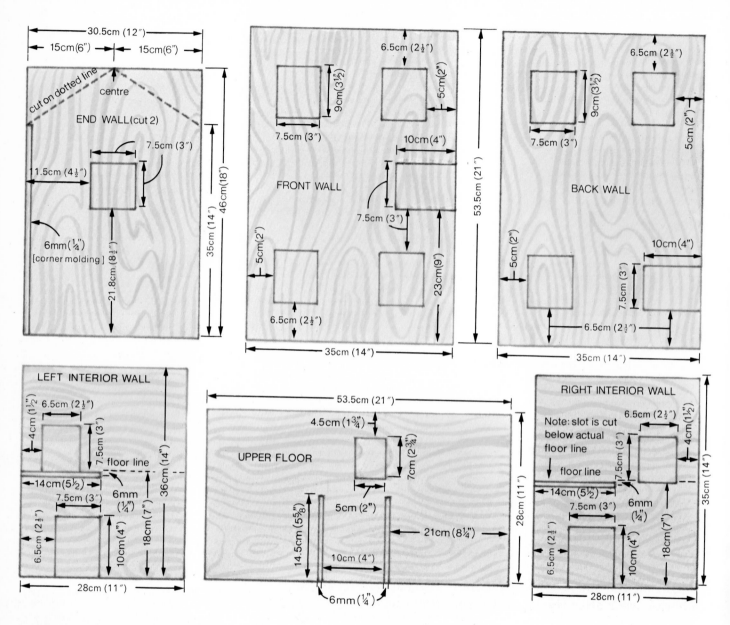

END WALL (cut 2)

30.5cm (12")
15cm (6") · 15cm (6")
cut on dotted line
centre
7.5cm (3")
11.5cm (4½")
46cm (18")
35cm (14")
21.8cm (8½")
6mm (¼")
[corner molding]

FRONT WALL

6.5cm (2½")
9cm (3½")
5cm (2")
7.5cm (3")
10cm (4")
7.5cm (3")
53.5cm (21")
5cm (2")
23cm (9")
6.5cm (2½")
35cm (14")

BACK WALL

6.5cm (2½")
9cm (3½")
5cm (2")
7.5cm (3")
5cm (2")
10cm (4")
7.5cm (3")
6.5cm (2½")
35cm (14")

LEFT INTERIOR WALL

6.5cm (2½")
4cm (1½")
7.5cm (3")
floor line
14cm (5½")
7.5cm (3")
6mm (¼")
36cm (14")
6.5cm (2½")
10cm (4")
18cm (7")
28cm (11")

UPPER FLOOR

53.5cm (21")
4.5cm (1¾")
7cm (2¾")
5cm (2")
14.5cm (5⅝")
21cm (8¼")
10cm (4")
28cm (11")
6mm (¼")

RIGHT INTERIOR WALL

Note: slot is cut below actual floor line
floor line
6.5cm (2½")
4cm (1½")
7.5cm (3")
14cm (5½")
6mm (¼")
7.5cm (3")
35cm (14")
6.5cm (2½")
10cm (4")
18cm (7")
28cm (11")

Above and opposite. Dimensions and marking out directions for the house.

Using the fret [copping] saw, make two cuts along the lines marking the slot. Cut out this centre piece by placing a chisel on the end line and tapping the chisel sharply with a mallet.

Mark out the doors on the interior walls and cut them out.

Now cut the corresponding slots in the floor. These are slightly deeper than the slots in the walls (see plan). Take care to align the walls with those on the floor. The small rectangle to be cut out is for the stairway and its edge should be in line with the inside edge of the right hand slot. Cut out using the fret [copping] saw.

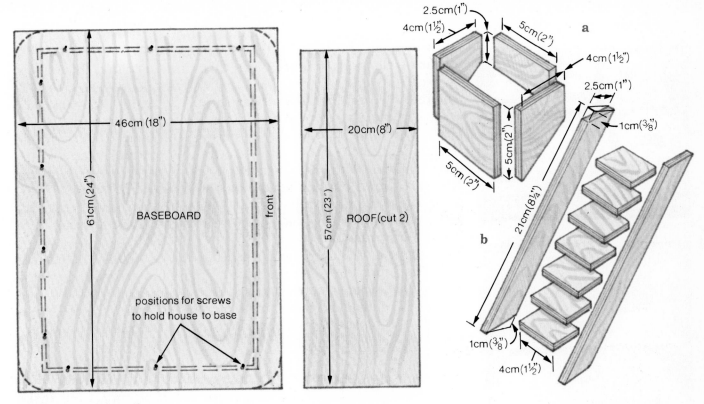

2.5cm(1")
4cm(1½")
5cm(2")
a
4cm(1½")
2.5cm(1")
1cm(⅜")
5cm(2")
5cm(2")
21cm(8¼")
b
1cm(⅜")
4cm(1½")

46cm (18")
61cm (24")
BASEBOARD
front

positions for screws
to hold house to base

20cm(8")
57cm (23")
ROOF(cut 2)

Painting interior

Before assembling the pieces it is advisable to prepare them for
painting. Plywood of this thickness has a tendency to split at the
edges where it has been sawn, leaving an untidy finish. To avoid
this, fill in these holes with wood filler. When the filler is dry, sand
the wood down with medium then fine grade glasspaper.

To seal the plywood, coat each surface with white primer. At this
stage you need only paint the interior of the house. Also paint the
base.

When dry, rub down with fine grade glasspaper before applying an
undercoat. Again sand this coat down when dry and finish with
an enamel paint that is non-toxic.

Assembly

The walls are now assembled and the house attached to the base.
Slot together the interior walls and floor and stand them on the
base (fig. 2). Next, lay the end walls on the table with the inside
surfaces uppermost.

On the left-hand edge of the left end wall, glue a 35cm (14in) strip
of quadrant beading [corner molding] (see plan). Glue a similar
strip to the right-hand edge of the right end wall.

These strips of beading [molding] form the guides which allow

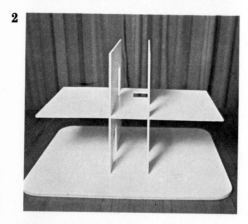

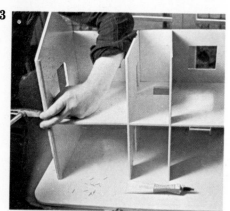

1. *The exterior walls.*
2. *Position of the interior walls.*
3. *Assembling the exterior walls.*
4. *Fitting the piano hinge.*
5. *Placing the chimney.*

the front of the house to slide out.

Lay the back wall on the table, inside surface uppermost. Place the interior wall-floor structure on to this, in the position that it is to be fixed.

The rectangle cut for the stairway should be nearest the back wall. Use a carpenter's square to check that all the edges are flush.

Draw a line lightly around the interior wall-floor structure where it butts against the back wall. Remove this structure and coat the marked lines with woodworking glue. Coat the edges of the structure, which butt against the back wall, as well.

With the back wall still lying flat, press the two glued edges together and turn the whole structure upright. Tack together with 1.3cm ($\frac{1}{2}$in) panel pins.

Hold the end walls in place against the interior wall-floor structure and check that the edges are flush. Draw lines around where the interior wall-floor structure butts against the end wall.

Repeat the gluing and nailing as shown in fig. 3 with the other end wall. The front wall should now slot between the beading [molding] and the inner wall structure.

Doors The two doors should now be cut from 6mm ($\frac{1}{4}$in) thick plywood. You can use the cut-outs from the doorways if they were not damaged. Cut them the size of the openings but make them 6mm ($\frac{1}{4}$in) shorter at the base. This allows a clearance for a small step to be glued to the baseboard. Paint the doors before hanging them with 1.3cm ($\frac{1}{2}$in) brass hinges.

Fixing house to base Position the house centrally on the base. Draw around the outer walls, both inside and out, with a pencil. Lift the house off the base and drill holes between the wall lines, as shown in the plan, with the 3mm ($\frac{1}{8}$in) bit. Countersink the holes from underneath the base. Fasten the house to the base with the 2.5cm (1in) No. 4 screws.

Having reached this point it is advisable to paint the outer surfaces of the house and base surround with primer undercoat and then with an enamel. Remember to paint the edges of the base.

The roof

The front of the roof is designed to fold back enabling children to reach the furniture on the upper floor. It also allows the front wall to slide out.

Take two pieces of plywood to be used for the roof and bevel one long edge of each. This is done with a plane and allows the roof to fold upwards when you wish to reach inside.

Fill any splits that may have occurred and then sand and paint the inner sides.

Lay the two pieces side by side, bevelled edges touching and facing down and screw the piano hinge into position (fig.4). If you are unable to find screws which do not go right through the wood, buy the shortest possible, screw straight through the wood and file down from the other side.

Place the roof section on the end wall supports. The two sections should lie snugly along the fall of the end walls with the bevelled edge uppermost and the hinge underneath. Make sure the front roof section folds back easily to allow the front section to slide out. Fix the back section of roof to the end walls with panel pins and finish the roof with enamel paint.

Making the chimney Cut four pieces of 6mm ($\frac{1}{4}$in) plywood to the dimensions shown in fig. A on the plan. Glue together.

Glue a small piece of cardboard on to the top of the chimney. Chimney pots, which can be cut from short lengths of plastic tubing, are fixed on to the cardboard.

When the chimney is assembled, paint it and glue to the roof 21.8cm ($8\frac{1}{2}$in) along from the left-hand end of the house (fig.5). The back of the chimney should be level with the edge of the bevel that you made on the apex of the roof.

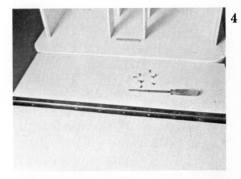

4

5

Porch, stairway and windows

The final components of the house are now made and fitted. The porch and stairs are cut from 6mm ($\frac{1}{4}$in) plywood.

Door surround or porch This should be made from three pieces of 6mm ($\frac{1}{4}$in) plywood, 2.5cm (1in) wide. Cut two pieces 11cm ($4\frac{1}{4}$in) long and a third 10cm (4in) long. Smooth with fine grade glasspaper, paint and glue to the area around the front of the door. The two longer pieces should be flush with the edges of the door opening, while the third piece forms the lintel with a slight overlap at each side.

To finish off the doors, screw small screws into them to form handles.

Making the stairs Cut two pieces of 6mm ($\frac{1}{4}$in) plywood, 21cm ($8\frac{1}{4}$in) long and 2.5cm (1in) wide (fig. B on the plan).

Measure 1cm ($\frac{3}{8}$in) from the top left-hand corner and bottom right-hand corner of each. Draw a line from this point to the adjacent corner and saw along this line. The steps must be set parallel to this sawn edge.

Cut seven steps from a piece of 6mm ($\frac{1}{4}$in) plywood, 2.5cm × 4cm (1in × 1$\frac{1}{2}$in).

Fasten to the side pieces with wood glue. Glue the stairway to the inside wall.

Window glazing The windows are easily made from clear plastic.

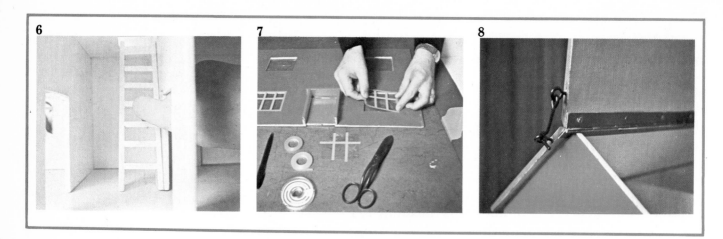

6. *Glue the stairway to the inside wall.*
7. *Attach the windows to the outside of the wall.*
8. *Screw a hook and eye catch to one end of the roof.*
9. *The finished house.*

The plastic used in packaging is ideal.

Cut the plastic 3mm ($\frac{1}{8}$in) larger than the window. Place the plastic flat on the table and, using the yellow adhesive tape, mark out the window panes. For the frames, use the orange tape. The tape used for the surrounds should overlap the plastic slightly in order to fasten the window to the outside of the wall (fig. 7).

Finally, screw a hook and eye catch to one end of the roof so that it will hold the front flap back when the roof is opened (fig. 8). The front of the house is then slid into position and the house is ready to be decorated (fig. 9).

Doll's house furniture

A doll's house, like any home, is not complete until it is furnished. You must consider the interior decor in relation to the style of the doll you have made or purchased. Furnishings can be miniature examples of the cabinet maker's art, or like the furnishings shown here, be simple shapes constructed from everyday materials. There are also kits available for making various styles of furniture.

In the past doll houses have been extremely elaborate affairs and as much of an interest for adults as for children. Many museums have exhibits of doll houses made for display more than play. Colleen Moore's doll house, on display in the Chicago Museum of Science and Industry, is perhaps one of the better known, with delicately wrought chandeliers, hand-woven carpets and furnishings made by the finest craftsmen of the era. Queen Mary's collection of doll houses is representative of several hundred years of architectural style and interior decoration.

Making simple furniture

The furniture shown here is made up from materials that would usually be thrown away, this means that pieces damaged in play can be easily and cheaply replaced. In fact, most of the furniture could be made by children as long as there is parental supervision to avoid cut fingers and too much mess.

Remember that the furniture is intended for children's play, scale is not overwhelmingly important, although a giant chair will look silly beside a tiny table.

Begin to collect things like eggboxes, yoghurt containers, plastic lids of varying sizes, cardboard tubes, pieces of polystyrene, scraps of fabric, lace and rug, large and small matchboxes and burned matches, buttons, beads, cotton reels of various sizes, reproductions of paintings from magazines and catalogues; these are the raw materials.

The best glue to use is a rubber-based adhesive; it dries quickly and any excess can be rubbed off. For polystyrene you must use polystyrene cement.

Furniture can be painted with spray paints, though care must be

Right: A fully furnished doll's house, everything built to the same scale.

taken not to use too much or the paint will run. Otherwise, use poster colours and then coat with a fixative when the paints are dry. For cutting the furniture shapes use a craft knife and a very sharp pair of nail scissors.

Armchair and sofa These are both made in the same way but use different size matchboxes; small boxes for armchairs and large for sofas.

To make an armchair use the inside of the box for the base (fig.1a) and the outer sleeve for the back (fig.1b). Cut away sections of the box as indicated. Glue the back to the base at a slight angle. When dry, paint the chair with poster colours.

To make cushions, cut pieces of foam to fit inside the seat and back of the chair. Coat each piece of foam with glue and then carefully fold a piece of fabric around each. Leave to dry and then glue the cushions into the chairs.

For the legs, make four holes in the base of the chair and trim four burned matches to 1.3cm ($\frac{1}{2}$in). Push the matches into the holes leaving the match heads exposed, then paint the match heads. Follow the same procedure for making a sofa, only use a larger matchbox.

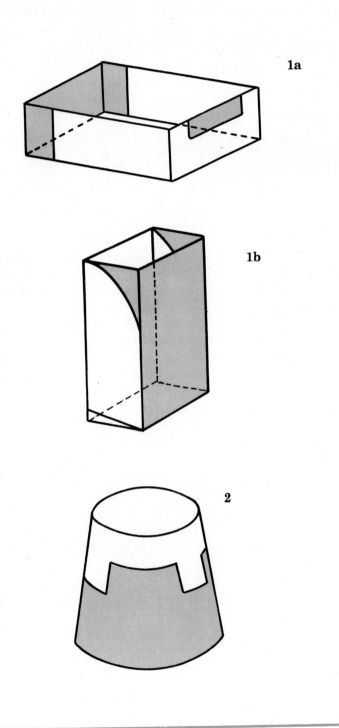

1a

1b

2

1a. Use the inside of the box for the base of the armchair.
1b. Use the outer sleeve for the back of the armchair.
2. A simple coffee table to make.

Coffee table This is made from a plastic yoghurt container. Using nail scissors, cut away part of the container indicated in fig.2. The bottom of the container is the top of the table. Colour with spray paint.

Carpet and curtains Pieces of heavy fabric such as corduroy, carpet offcuts, and scraps of fur can all be used for floor coverings. The two rugs shown here are made from needlework canvas; one piece has been worked in tapestry wool and the other coloured with felt pens. Scraps of lace, gingham or other cotton fabrics can be used to make window curtains also, offcuts from cane blinds can be used for window coverings.

Side table This is made from a cotton reel covered with a circle of fabric glued firmly to the top of the reel and caught to the sides of the reel with small spots of glue.

Dining room

Table Use, if possible, a very large cotton reel (obtainable from an upholsterer or tailor) for the base. Paint the reel and when dry glue a jar lid to one end. Then cover the lid with a circular piece of cloth glued to the top and sides of the lid.

Chairs Use a cup section from an egg box for each chair. Cut away as indicated in fig.3. The chairs can be painted or left their natural colour as the chairs shown here. The legs are made from matchsticks pushed through the seat of the chairs and held in place with small dabs of glue. As the chairs are very light, it is best to make the seat cushions by covering a coin with fabric. Glue the cushions to the seat.

Kitchen

These are all constructed in the same manner; from matchboxes cut in half and covered with thin cardboard.

Cupboard Cut a large matchbox sleeve cover in half across the width. Cut a top for the cupboard from a piece of cardboard slightly larger than the open end of the matchbox. Cut two doors in the front of the box, leaving the hinged sides uncut. Score the hinged sides so that they will fold forward easily. Glue the top piece and then paint the entire cupboard with spray paint. Paint and insert matchhead handles in the door fronts.

Stove Use the remaining half matchbox to make the stove. Cut two pieces of cardboard to cover the sides and another piece to cover the top – large enough to accommodate the four buttons that are used to represent the cooking rings. Cut the oven door as for the cupboard doors. Cut a window in the oven door. Now glue the cardboard sides and top to the box and paint with spray

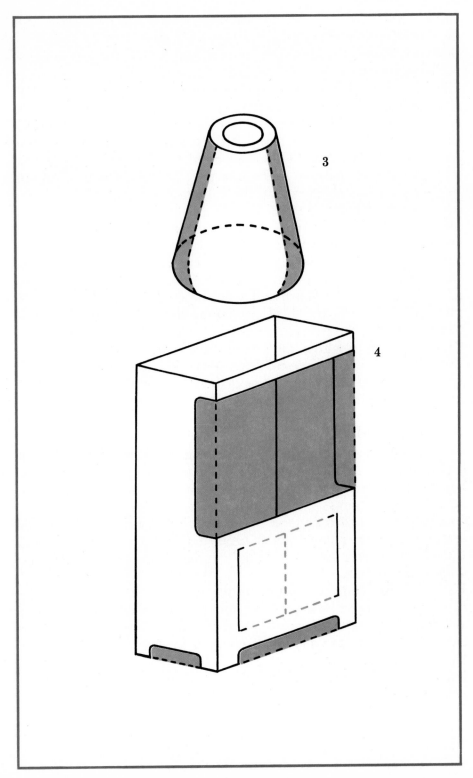

3. *How to make chairs from egg boxes.*
4. *A dresser from the sleeve of a large matchbox.*

paints. Glue four buttons to the top and a piece of acetate over the wrong side of the window to represent glass.

Sink unit This is made from another half matchbox sleeve cover with a door cut in the front to one side, opposite the sink position. Cut three pieces of card as for the stove. Take one cup section from an egg box and cut the top two-thirds away leaving a shallow cup. Cut a circle at one end of the top cardboard piece to match the circumference of the cup. Glue the sides and top to the box and then paint the unit. Glue a piece of foil into the egg box and then glue it into the hole in the unit top. This is the sink. You will have to cut out a semicircle in the back of the box to allow for the depth and width of the sink.

Dresser This is made from a whole matchbox sleeve cover. Cut away the sections shown in fig.4 and cut doors as for cupboard. Cut three pieces of cardboard: two to cover the top and bottom and one to form the bottom shelf, allowing 6mm ($\frac{1}{4}$in) along the long edges of each piece. Score and fold the extra 6mm ($\frac{1}{4}$in) on each piece of cardboard to one side. Position in the box and glue these to the inside of the cover.

Cut shelves to fit within the box and then cut matchstick brackets to the depth of the shelves. Glue a bracket to the ends of each shelf. Glue the shelves into position and paint the dresser. Then fix two small pieces of matchstick as knobs on the cupboard.

Entrance hall

Coat hanger and umbrella stand Insert a pencil into the inside of a plastic cotton reel. Make little holes with a bradawl along the length of the pencil and glue small lengths of matchstick into each hole. Paint the hanger to match the cotton reel base.

Lampshades Shades can be made from the bottom of egg box sections or from pleated paper candy cups. Put a piece of thread through the centre and fix the shade to the ceiling of the doll house with a dab of glue.

For a standing lamp use a button for the base, first removing the centre holes of the button by melting through the holes or sawing out the centres with a fret (copping) saw. Insert a plastic straw into the hole, cut it to the appropriate length for the stand and make a shade as described above.

Mirrors or paintings Use the lid of a small plastic container, paint the edges and then paste either a picture or a piece of silver foil into the centre.

Master bedroom

Double bed Cut a piece of cardboard to the size of the bed required. Cut a piece of 2.5cm (1in) deep foam to the size of the cardboard. Cut a small strip of foam to represent pillows and glue to the mattress piece. Glue the card to the mattress bottom and then cover the entire bed with a piece of fabric glued in place.

Dressing table Cut a plastic lid in half and glue to a cotton reel base. Cut a semi-circle of fabric large enough to cover the lid and reach the floor and glue in place over the lid. Make a mirror from a smaller lid; cut away roughly $\frac{1}{4}$ of the lid and then paint it to co-ordinate with the tablecloth. When the paint is dry, glue a circle of foil into the lid recess to represent a mirror.

Wardrobe This is made from the outside sleeve cover of a large matchbox. The doors are cut as before, scoring the hinged sides so that they fold out easily. Cut away the parts of the box as shown in fig.5. The top of the wardrobe and the base are cut to size from the inside of the box and glued into place. Paint the wardrobe and fix matchhead handles in place.

Children's room

Cradle Use the cardboard tube from a lavatory roll. Cut away the areas indicated in fig.6. Cut two strips of thin cardboard 6mm ($\frac{1}{4}$in) wide and long enough to fit the inner circumference of the tube. Glue in place just inside each end of the tube with the outer edges flush. Cut two circles of cardboard the size of the tube openings and then glue the circles over the ends, fixing them to the cardboard collars fitted inside. Paint with spray paint.

For the bedding, use a small piece of foam cut to fit within the cradle and covered with fabric.

Playpen For the base use the inside of a large matchbox and a piece of fabric covered foam for the mattress. For the sides use an offcut of cane blind glued between the mattress and the inner edge of the box. Matchsticks or toothpicks with pointed ends removed could also be used for the sides of the playpen.

Chest of drawers Glue four small matchboxes one on top of the other. Cover the sides and top with thin cardboard cut to fit.

Use matchheads for handles. Take the inside of another small matchbox and cut away each side so that the corners of the box remain to represent legs. Glue this to the bottom of the drawer unit as a base.

Bathroom

Bath Use the inside of a large matchbox for the exterior of the bath and a moulded plastic wrapper of the type used in the packaging of model cars. Paint the outside of the matchbox. Leave to dry and then glue the plastic wrapper into the box.

5. A wardrobe made from the sleeve of a large matchbox.
6. Even the cardboard tube from a lavatory roll can be made use of. Here is a very simple but charming cradle to make.

Wash basin Cut one cup section of an egg box and glue the base to the end of a thin plastic cotton reel. Make the sink surround from a square piece of thin cardboard cut 1.3cm ($\frac{1}{2}$in) larger all round than the circumference of the cup section. Cut a hole in the centre of the cardboard to fit the cup; round off two adjacent corners to make the front of the wash basin and then glue the cardboard surround to the cup section. Paint to match the bath, or leave it its natural colour.

Toilet This is made from two cup sections of an egg box plus a piece of egg box lid. For the base cut one cup in half, and for the bowl use the bottom third of the cup. For the lid use a piece of the box top cut to fit the circumference of the bowl and with a small tab left at the back to serve as a hinge. Glue the tab to the back of the bowl and glue the bowl to the bottom of the base piece. Paint to match the basin and bath or leave it its natural colour.

Doll's clothes

Making costume dolls

Choosing a theme for costume dolls

Dressing costume dolls is an appealing craft for anyone who likes to work in miniature and finds enjoyment in improvising for detailed effects. A collection can be built up according to one's particular interest: historical costumes provide an opportunity for working with rich fabrics, sequins and beads, while national costumes offer scope for embroidery. Theatrical costumes are another idea for a collection, choosing clothes worn by famous actors and actresses, or one might decide to build a collection of twentieth century fashion.

Selecting a suitable doll

It is important to choose dolls which can be obtained fairly easily, particularly when a collection is being started. Dolls with an adult look are essential – it is very difficult to make a baby doll look anything but a baby – and if special poses are required choose one with adjustable limbs. The dressed dolls shown here are of one particular type, and it can be seen that they seem to take on different features once the costume is on them.

This particular range of doll is made in such a way that the arms, legs, and head can be easily removed to simplify dressing.

Fabrics and effects

It is very important indeed to use fabrics in scale with the doll. Look for fabrics with this clearly in mind. Small prints and fine weaves will give a dressed doll a more realistic look, and if the desired print isn't available use a plain fabric and paint the design. Fabrics can be painted with gold, silver, poster paints or inks after they have been constructed. Alternatively, felt pens or fabric paints can be used to paint the fabrics before they are made up [finished]. Short cuts can be used to achieve the final effect, such as gluing on details like sequins, feathers or trimmings, but use a good adhesive that will dry clear.

Search out and keep miniature trims of all kinds: broken necklaces for jewels, ribbon, lace edging, rouleau [rolled] trimming and tiny

Left: An ordinary doll dressed in Elizabethan costume. Instructions are given for making everything from the underskirt to the wing veil and ruffle.

buttons all help to build up the effect. Silver paper, foil, paper doilies in white, silver and gold, feathers, scraps of wool, pieces of tinsel, and even gift wrapping paper should be in your store of pieces. Wherever possible choose fabrics which do not fray easily. Felt, of course, is good, and so is non-woven interfacing; the latter can be painted or sprayed and is very good for making hats and other accessories. Don't, however, reject velvet, silk and satin as fabrics simply because they fray – they do add tremendous richness to costumes. Rather, handle these materials carefully and don't cut seams too closely.

Ideas for costumes and making patterns

Once the theme for the collection has been decided upon, try to find colour pictures or drawings to work from. Study the reference carefully and get the essential line of the dress firmly in mind. One characteristic of the garment will stand out – in the Elizabethan doll's costume, for instance, it is the ruff and collar. Try to find out what the back of the costume looks like – this is rather important.

Cut patterns for the garment pieces in newspaper, pinning them onto the doll for fit, remembering to allow for seams. Costume dolls are rarely undressed so it isn't necessary to consider openings and fastenings.

Once sewing has started, it is usually easier to sew sections directly onto the doll. A better fit is achieved in this way and if one section goes wrong it can easily be removed.

Elizabethan costume

Underskirt From stiff white nylon, cut a rectangle 46cm × 18cm (18in × 7in). Mark the underskirt fabric as indicated, leaving 6mm ($\frac{1}{4}$in) seam allowance. The area to be pleated should fall over the doll's hips. Pleat the fabric very closely and stitch into position.

Finish the waist with seam binding leaving 15cm (6in) at each end for tying.

Turn up and stitch a 1cm ($\frac{3}{8}$in) hem and sew on lace.

Sew centre back seam, leaving 4cm ($1\frac{1}{2}$in) waist opening.

Dress From brocade, cut one 46cm × 20cm (18in × 8in) rectangle for the skirt. Cut another rectangle 32cm × 5cm ($12\frac{1}{2}$in × 2in) for the farthingale [hooped petticoat].

Cut one bodice front, two bodice backs, two sleeves and one stomacher from non-woven interfacing.

Stitch the darts in the front and back bodice pieces. Stitch the shoulder seams and turn in the neck edge, stitching close to the edge.

Insert sleeves into armholes taking in the fullness at top of each sleeve with small pleats. Stitch sleeves to armholes. Close side and sleeve seams. Turn up 3mm ($\frac{1}{8}$in) hem on each sleeve and stitch close to edge.

Stitch seam in the skirt back leaving 4cm ($1\frac{1}{2}$in) open at top. Pleat the skirt in similar way to the underskirt and, with right sides facing, stitch the skirt to the bodice.

Turn in back facing stitching close to edge and sew on press studs [snap fasteners]. Turn up 6mm ($\frac{1}{4}$in) hem on skirt and finish with two parallel rows of stitching.

**Elizabethan costume
for 30.5cm (12in) doll**

You will need:
20cm (8in) of 90cm (35in) wide brocade.
20cm × 50cm (8in × 20in) piece of stiff white nylon.
102cm (40in) of 2cm ($\frac{3}{4}$in) wide lace
40.5cm (16in) of seam binding.
Piece of white net 10cm × 50cm (4in × 20in).
Glass and pearl beads.
50cm (20in) narrow gold trim.
2 snap fastenings.
Florists wire.
Scrap of non-woven interfacing.

Left: The finished costume, which can be matched in every detail if you follow the instructions carefully.

To make the farthingale [hooped petticoat], take the 32cm × 5cm (12½in × 2in) rectangle and stitch a 6mm (¼in) hem on three raw edges. Run a gathering thread along the remaining raw edge and pull up the gathers until the farthingale [petticoat] fits the dress waistline. Stitch the farthingale [petticoat] to the dress.

Stomacher Stitch together the non-woven interfacing and brocade stomachers. Turn raw edge of the brocade to the wrong side of the stomacher and stitch in place close to the edge. Decorate with pearl beads and sew gold trim to the top edge. Stitch the stomacher to the bodice front.

Wing veil and ruffle For the ruffle cut four 12cm × 4cm (4¾in × 1½in) rectangles in net. Using the pattern, cut four wing veils in net.

Take two rectangles and stitch together along two long and one short side. Attach lace to one long edge and turn back remaining short edge. Pleat and sew ruffle to neckline between back opening and top corners of the stomacher, stitching down the short edge at the shoulder edge.

Take two wing veil pieces and stitch them together overcasting the raw edges. Decorate edges with beads of varying size. Attach to the back bodice of the dress at the shoulders.

Repeat for other wing veil.

Crown Thread beads onto florist's wire and join the ends to form a circle. Take two pieces of florist's wire and thread each with beads. Fasten them together at the centre by twisting one around the other. Twist each end around the wire circle and bend to desired shape. Stitch tear-drop bead in centre.

Make a long pearl necklace by threading pearl beads to desired length.

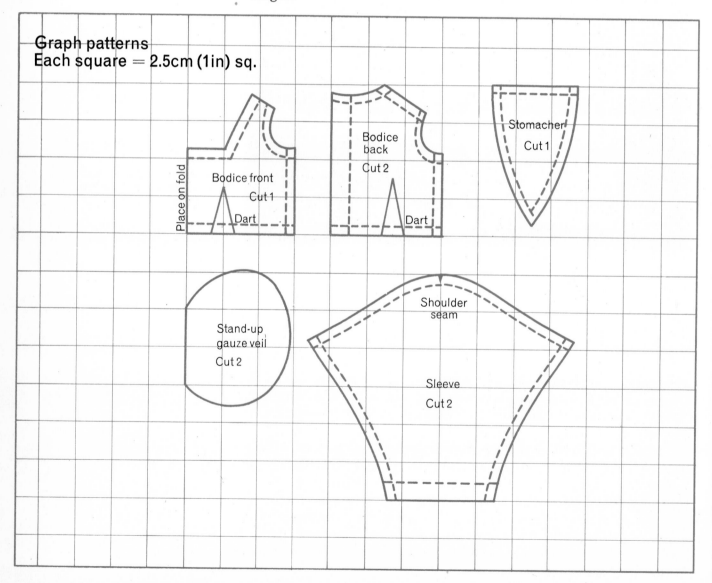

Graph patterns
Each square = 2.5cm (1in) sq.

Place on fold

Bodice front
Cut 1
Dart

Bodice back
Cut 2
Dart

Stomacher
Cut 1

Stand-up gauze veil
Cut 2

Shoulder seam

Sleeve
Cut 2

Polish costume

Skirt Cut a rectangle 50cm × 13cm (20in × 5in) and another 13cm × 2.5cm (5in × 1in) from brightly coloured cotton material. Turn up 2cm (¾in) hem and stitch along one long edge.

Pin two parellel rows of ribbon near hemline and then stitch in place close to ribbon edges.

Stitch a row of gathering threads along the remaining long edge. Take a 1cm (⅜in) centre back seam and leave a 1.3cm (½in) waist opening at the top. Pull up gathers to fit the doll's waist.

Using the smaller rectangle and with right sides facing, make a waistband by stitching the short ends together. Turn to right side

Polish costume for 30.5cm (12in) doll
You will need: Piece of brightly coloured plain cotton material 50cm × 30.5cm (20in × 12in). Piece of white cotton material 40.5cm × 10cm (16in × 4in). Piece of white nylon 50cm × 30.5cm (20in × 12in). Small square of black velvet. 102cm (40in) of 6mm (¼in) wide ribbon in red, yellow and green. 102cm (40in) of 1.3cm (½in) wide lace. 4 eyelets. Length of black embroidery thread and fine crochet hook. Round elastic. Thin cardboard. 3 press studs [snap fasteners]. Small artificial flowers. Shirring elastic. Clear drying glue.

Left: The finished costume.

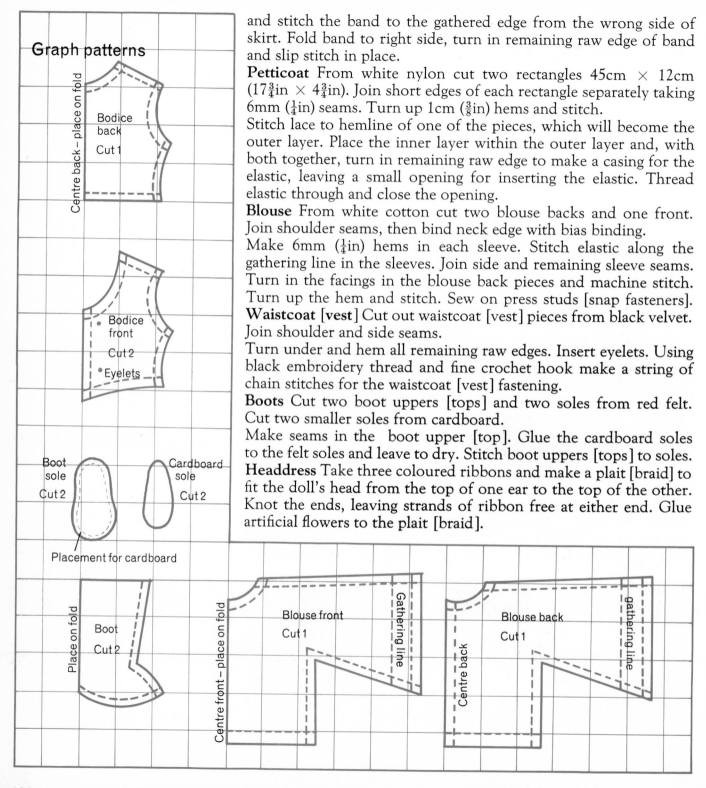

Graph patterns

Centre back – place on fold

Bodice back
Cut 1

Bodice front
Cut 2
• Eyelets

Boot sole
Cut 2

Cardboard sole
Cut 2

Placement for cardboard

Place on fold

Boot
Cut 2

Centre front – place on fold

Blouse front
Cut 1

Gathering line

Centre back

Blouse back
Cut 1

gathering line

and stitch the band to the gathered edge from the wrong side of skirt. Fold band to right side, turn in remaining raw edge of band and slip stitch in place.

Petticoat From white nylon cut two rectangles 45cm × 12cm (17¾in × 4¾in). Join short edges of each rectangle separately taking 6mm (¼in) seams. Turn up 1cm (⅜in) hems and stitch.

Stitch lace to hemline of one of the pieces, which will become the outer layer. Place the inner layer within the outer layer and, with both together, turn in remaining raw edge to make a casing for the elastic, leaving a small opening for inserting the elastic. Thread elastic through and close the opening.

Blouse From white cotton cut two blouse backs and one front. Join shoulder seams, then bind neck edge with bias binding.

Make 6mm (¼in) hems in each sleeve. Stitch elastic along the gathering line in the sleeves. Join side and remaining sleeve seams. Turn in the facings in the blouse back pieces and machine stitch. Turn up the hem and stitch. Sew on press studs [snap fasteners].

Waistcoat [vest] Cut out waistcoat [vest] pieces from black velvet. Join shoulder and side seams.

Turn under and hem all remaining raw edges. Insert eyelets. Using black embroidery thread and fine crochet hook make a string of chain stitches for the waistcoat [vest] fastening.

Boots Cut two boot uppers [tops] and two soles from red felt. Cut two smaller soles from cardboard.

Make seams in the boot upper [top]. Glue the cardboard soles to the felt soles and leave to dry. Stitch boot uppers [tops] to soles.

Headdress Take three coloured ribbons and make a plait [braid] to fit the doll's head from the top of one ear to the top of the other. Knot the ends, leaving strands of ribbon free at either end. Glue artificial flowers to the plait [braid].

Making patterns

Whether you have made a doll or purchased one, she will surely need a wardrobe, as a major part of a child's pleasure in playing with these toys is derived from dressing dolly to suit the play activity—from tea parties to a walk in the rain.

Commercial patterns for doll clothes can be purchased, but it is very simple and much cheaper to make your own. Begin with something simple, keeping to basic shapes and using fabric offcuts or cast-off clothes for fabric. Buttons, beads from a broken necklace and scraps of ribbon and lace can be used to trim the garments; small pieces of soft leather are useful for making shoes and tiny handbags—the simplest designs will be enhanced by trimmings of some kind.

The pattern shapes are based on the doll's torso, so it is necessary to draw a template on which to fashion the pattern pieces. To do this, divide the torso pattern piece in half lengthways and trace around it on a piece of cardboard, eliminating seam allowances (fig.1). Note the measurements indicated, depth and width (the latter is half the total of the torso pattern piece).

If you are making patterns for a purchased doll you will have to trace around the doll's torso and then take the necessary measurements from the doll, adding the difference in width equally to both sides of the traced outline, thus allowing for the change from a three-dimensional shape to a two-dimensional one.

With the template completed, you can begin pattern designing.

Fix a piece of tracing paper over the template so that it will not slip about and on it sketch the shape of the desired garment. Keep in mind where the pattern can be placed on the fabric fold and where seams and facings will be, there adding seam allowances to the pattern piece. Also allow a little extra room for ease when dressing the doll. Most dolls have fairly large heads, so when shaping neck openings this must be allowed for.

Underwear
Fig. 2 shows a pattern for a simple petticoat and has been drawn

over the template. Underwear such as panties and petticoats fit more closely than outerwear and therefore follow the shape of the body more distinctly. Note that the neckline of the petticoat falls roughly halfway between the bottom of the shoulder and base of the armhole.

Dresses

Patterns for smock-type dresses, pinafores [jumpers] and dresses with a fitted bodice and gathered or pleated skirt are made on the same principle. Figs. 3 and 4 show respectively a bodice pattern

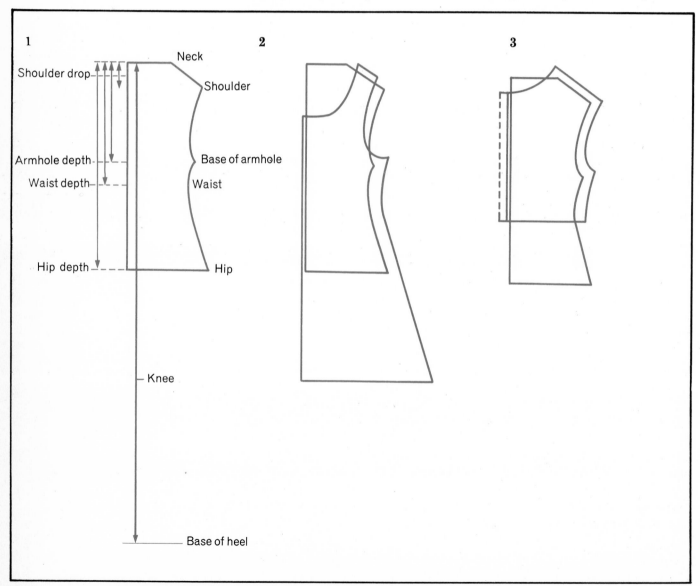

and ways of altering the basic shape with trims and openings. Neck-lines can be round, square or V-shaped. For inspiration, and as a reference for pattern shapes, it is worthwhile having a look at commercial patterns for doll's and even children's clothes.

To determine fabric requirements for a dress with gathers at either the waistline or on to a yoke, double the width measurement to allow enough fullness. For a pleated skirt the width will be three times the measurement you are fitting.

Skirts

A gathered skirt can be made using two rectangles of fabric; their size determined by the desired finished length plus hem allowance, and double the waist measurement plus seam allowances. Gather the skirt on to a waistband or, alternatively, stitch a casing for elastic to be threaded through, in which case you must allow for turning at the waist edge as well as at the hem. Elastic is probably the easiest way to finish the waist as it is less fiddly and also easier than buttons for a small child to manipulate.

Circular skirts are made by drawing a circle with a radius larger than the required finished length of the skirt. Cut out the circle, fold it evenly into four and trim $\frac{1}{4}$ of the total waist measurement at the apex (fig. 5a). Unfold the circle and use as a pattern. Cut the waist opening on the straight of grain, finishing it and the waistline with bias binding and a hook and eye fastening.

The pattern for a gored skirt is made in the same manner, except that seam allowances must be added to each gore (fig. 5b). The number of gores may be varied according to how the circle is divided.

Shoes

Use the foot pattern for drawing the template. Remember that the shoes will fit over the foot, so allow an extra 6mm ($\frac{1}{4}$in) all round the sole pattern piece. If you wish to make boots, the width and length of the leg from knee down must also be taken into consideration.

It is best to use felt or soft leather scraps for footwear as these materials do not fray and you will not have to worry about hiding seams.

Blouses

Although it is possible to make a blouse with set-in sleeves you will, in all likelihood, find this is a chore. Therefore, try to incorporate the sleeves into the body of the blouse. Fig. 6 gives a shape for a blouse with full sleeves gathered at the wrist.

1. *Basic mould of a doll's body for pattern making.*
2. *A basic pattern for a petticoat.*
3. *A basic pattern for a dress bodice; the dotted line indicates the extra allowance for facings at the back or front.*

4. *Ways of altering the basic shape of the bodice.*
5a. *Pattern for a circular skirt.*
5b. *Pattern for a gored skirt.*
6. *The shape for a blouse with full sleeves gathered at the wrist.*

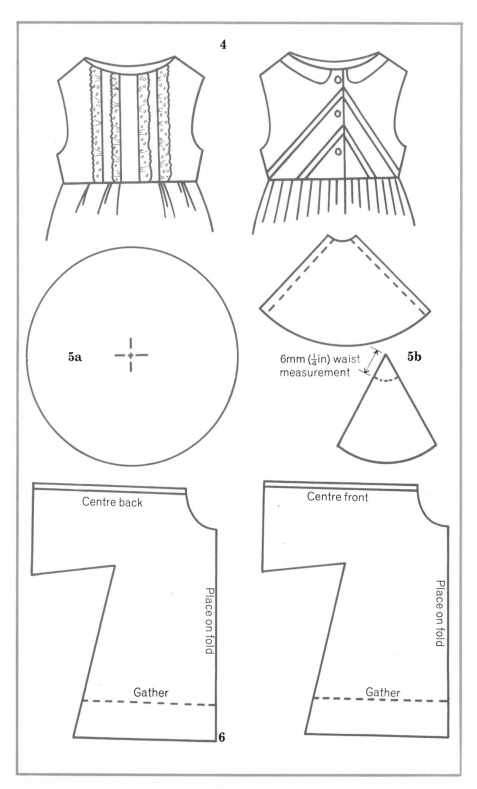

A basic wardrobe

Petticoat and panties for 35cm (14in) doll
You will need: White cotton material 30.5cm × 50cm (12in × 20in). 30.5cm × 4.5cm (12in × 1¾in) wide pre-gathered broderie anglaise [eyelet] trimming. 24cm × 1cm (9½in × ⅜in) wide lace. White bias binding. 10cm (4in) length of 1cm (⅜in) wide ribbon. Sewing thread.

Left: All the clothes featured in this chapter are made to fit a 35cm (14in) doll.

Petticoat and panties

Petticoat From white cotton material cut out petticoat front and back alike. Turn under 6mm (¼in) along top edge of each piece and sew narrow broderie anglaise [eyelet] trim to this turning. Repeat for other side.

Join the side seams and bind the armholes with bias binding. Turn under 6mm ($\frac{1}{4}$in) hem allowance and stitch the 4.5cm ($1\frac{3}{4}$in) wide broderie anglaise [eyelet] trimming around the bottom. Stitch ribbon to front and back to form shoulder straps.

Panties Cut out and bind the leg edges with bias binding. Join side seams. Make a 1cm ($\frac{3}{8}$in) hem [casing] along the top edge. Leave one end open and thread elastic through this. Close the opening. Stitch lace around each leg edge.

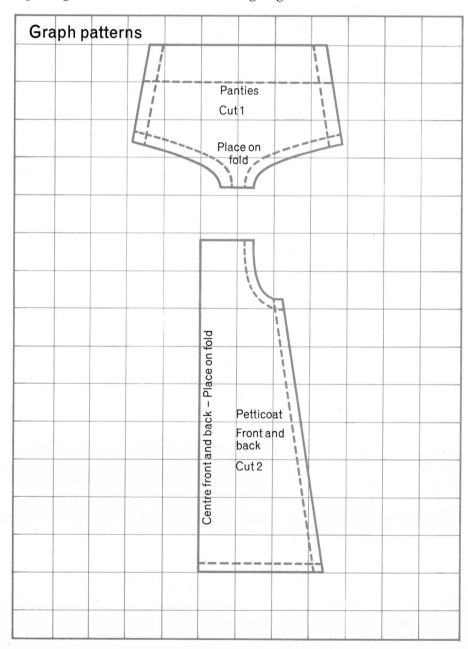

Graph patterns

Panties
Cut 1

Place on fold

Centre front and back – Place on fold

Petticoat
Front and back
Cut 2

Skirt and blouse

Start by cutting a 4cm (1½in) wide strip from each selvage for the skirt frill. (Using the selvage in this way dispenses with a hem.) Cut a 12cm × 32cm (4¾in × 12½in) rectangle for the skirt. Cut out the blouse pieces using the pattern provided.

Skirt Make a 6mm (¼in) seam in the centre back of the skirt rectangle. Along the raw edge make a 6mm (¼in) deep casing for elastic and stitch along top and bottom close to edges.

Stitch two frill pieces together along short edges.

Run a gathering thread 6mm (¼in) away from the long raw edge. Pull up the gathers so that the frill fits the skirt hem. Distribute the gathers evenly and pin in place. Stitch the gathers. Insert elastic into waist.

Blouse Join the centre front seam, leaving open above notch. Sew all armhole seams. Stitch along the gathering line all round the neck edge. Pull up the gathers until the neck measures 17cm (6¾in). Bind the neck edge with bias binding, spacing gathers evenly and leaving 15cm (6in) spare at each end for tying. Stitch sleeves and side seams. Turn up hem allowance and stitch.

Skirt and blouse for 35cm (14in) doll
You will need: 30.5cm (12in) of 90cm (35in) wide cotton fabric. Bias binding. Round elastic. Sewing thread.

Left: The finished skirt and blouse – made-to-measure for the 35cm (14in) doll described on pages 16-17.

129

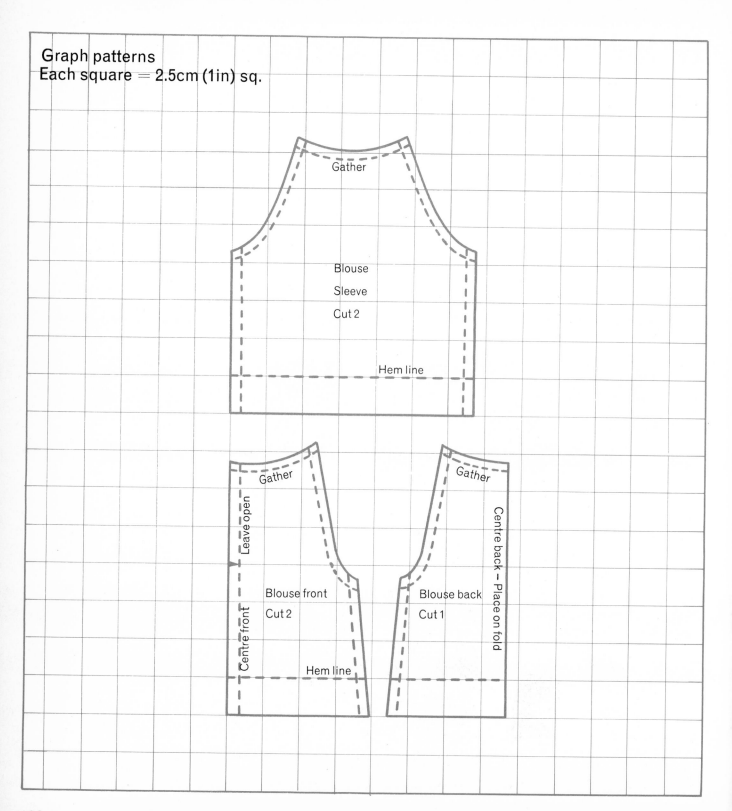

Graph patterns
Each square = 2.5cm (1in) sq.

Gather

Blouse

Sleeve

Cut 2

Hem line

Gather

Gather

Leave open

Centre front

Centre back – Place on fold

Blouse front

Cut 2

Blouse back

Cut 1

Hem line

Duffle coat
for 35cm (14in) doll

You will need:
Piece of brightly coloured felt
30.5cm × 50cm (12in × 20in)
4 toggle fasteners.
Thread to match felt.

*Left: This coat and matching pair
of boots are quite quick and
simple to make.*

Duffle coat

Cut out two fronts, one back, two sleeves, two pockets, two
toggle flaps and one hood from the felt.

Stitch pockets to fronts on the positions shown on the pattern
pieces.

Taking 6mm ($\frac{1}{4}$in) seams throughout, join sleeves to armholes
then sew side seams and underarm sleeve seams with one line of
stitching. Join the seam in the hood and fit the hood to the neck
line, matching centre back to hood seam.

Stitch toggle flaps to right front so that half the flap hangs over the
coat opening. Make a small slash in the overhang for use as a
buttonhole.

As this garment is made in felt there is no need to make hems.

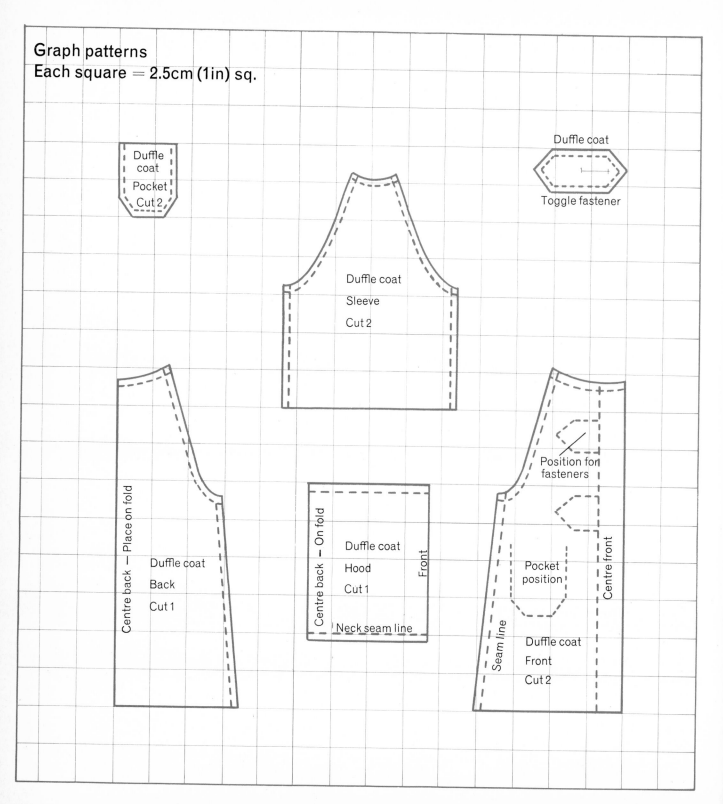

Graph patterns
Each square = 2.5cm (1in) sq.

Duffle coat
Pocket
Cut 2

Duffle coat

Toggle fastener

Duffle coat
Sleeve
Cut 2

Centre back — Place on fold

Duffle coat
Back
Cut 1

Centre back — On fold

Duffle coat
Hood
Cut 1

Neck seam line

Front

Position for fasteners

Pocket
position

Seam line

Centre front

Duffle coat
Front
Cut 2

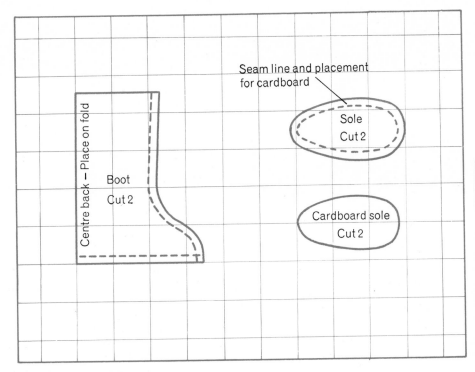

Wellington boots

You will need:
Small piece of wet-look vinyl.
10cm (4in) square of black felt.
Thin cardboard.
Fabric glue.
Sewing thread.

Dressing gown [robe]
for 35cm (14in) doll

You will need:
Piece of quilted fabric 30.5cm ×
50cm (12in × 20in).
3 small buttons.
3 press studs [snap fasteners].
Matching sewing thread.

Wellington boots

Cut two Wellington boot uppers [tops] from wet-look vinyl and two soles from black felt. Cut two smaller soles from cardboard. Make the seam in the upper [top] with right sides together. Clip the seam where it curves.

Glue the cardboard sole on to the black felt sole with fabric glue and leave to dry.

With right sides together, sew upper [top] to sole, once again clipping around the curves. Turn inside out.

Dressing gown [robe]

Cut out two fronts, one back, two sleeves and one collar from quilted fabric. Taking 1cm ($\frac{3}{8}$in) seams throughout, join the shoulder seams. With right sides together, pin sleeve head [cap] into armhole and stitch. Repeat with other sleeve.

Turn under 6mm ($\frac{1}{4}$in) hem on curved edge of collar and stitch. Fit collar to neck opening matching centre backs and front notches. Stitch in place. Overcast seam allowance so that the collar will stand up. Join side and underarm seams.

Turn under front facings and hem in position. Turn up and stitch hems on sleeves and bottom edge.

Sew buttons onto right side of dressing gown [robe] and press studs [snap fasteners] to correspond to button positions.

Nightdress [Nightgown]
35cm (14in) doll

You will need:
30.5cm (12in) of 90cm (35in) wide
nylon seersucker or suitable
equivalent fabric.
40cm (16in) of 2.5cm (1in) wide
trimming.
2 rosebud trims.
1 press stud [snap fastener].
Polyester sewing thread.

*Right: A beautiful nightdress and
quilted dressing gown complete
the doll's wardrobe.*

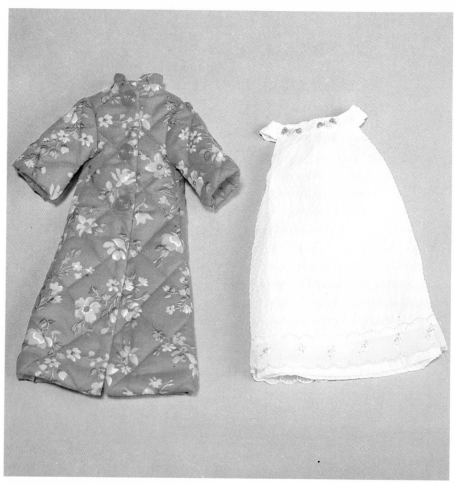

Nightdress [nightgown]

Cut out all pattern pieces from seersucker. Taking 6mm ($\frac{1}{4}$in)
seams throughout, take one top layer and one under layer of
nightdress [nightgown] skirt and, with right sides together, sew the
armholes. Turn inside out. Gather along the top neck edge. Repeat
this process for the other pieces of nightdress [nightgown] skirt.
Pull up gathers to fit inside the notches on the front and back yoke
pieces. Stitch the gathers into position. Join one shoulder seam.
Also join one shoulder seam in yoke facing. Stitch yoke facing to
yoke around neck edge, matching shoulder seams. Turn under
and hem any raw edges.

Stitch together the side seams of the top and under layers of the
nightdress [nightgown]. Then make 1cm ($\frac{3}{8}$in) hems in both
top and under skirt. Stitch trim to upper layer of nightdress
[nightgown] along the hemmed edge. Sew on rosebud trims to
yoke and press studs [snap fasteners] at one shoulder.

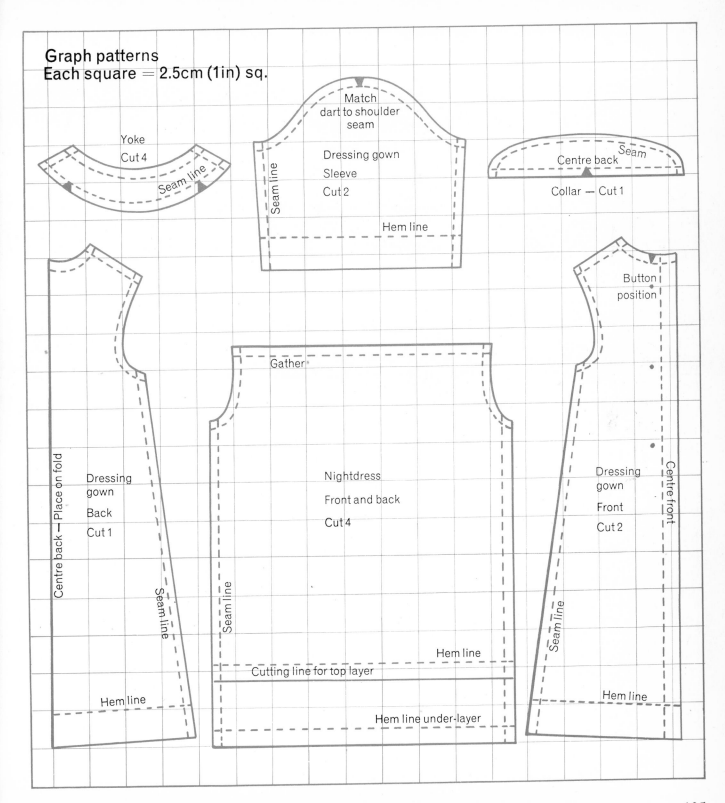

Graph patterns
Each square = 2.5cm (1in) sq.

Yoke
Cut 4

Seam line

Match
dart to shoulder
seam

Dressing gown
Sleeve
Cut 2

Seam line

Hem line

Centre back

Seam

Collar — Cut 1

Button
position

Gather

Centre back — Place on fold

Dressing
gown
Back
Cut 1

Seam line

Hem line

Nightdress

Front and back

Cut 4

Seam line

Hem line

Cutting line for top layer

Hem line under-layer

Dressing
gown
Front
Cut 2

Centre front

Seam line

Hem line

Index

Artwork

Barbara Firth: 18, 20L, 22L, 46, 47
Douglas Hall: 36
Malcolm Hatton: 8/9, 28/9, 62, 70/1, 77,
    86/7, 94, 95, 109, 111, 114, 120, 122, 124,
    126, 128, 130, 132, 133, 135
Rosemary Hoar: 2, 4, 13
Valentine Hoar: 7, 11
John Hutchinson: 20/1, 22B, 26, 27, 30, 34,
    40, 41, 42, 43, 80, 81
Susan Ives: 17
Trevor Lawrence: 15, 23, 99
Coral Mula: 76
Paul Williams: 48, 49, 50BL, 53, 54, 84, 102,
    103

Picture credits

Steve Bicknell: 74/5, 76CL
Stuart Dalby: 104, 105TL, 106
Ray Duns: 77
Leslie Fox: 11
Geoffrey Frosh: 67BR, 85
Melvin Grey: 50BR, 68/9
Peter Heinz: 61, 62T
Jeany: 100
Paul Kemp: 60, 106B
Chris Lewis: 45
Dick Miller: 62B, 63L
Julian Nieman: 39, 40TL
Alastair Ogilvie: 7
Peter Pugh-Cook: 19, 25, 32/3, 78/9
Jerry Tubby: 99T
Mike Wells: 52, 57, 58, 59